IRELAND

DENMARK

ENGLAND

NORTH SEA

London

NETHERLANDS

BELGIUM

GERM.

RHINE

Paris SEINE

LOIRE

FRANCE

Constance

SWITZERLAND

Geneva

AU

Lyons
Vienne

Trent

BAY OF
BISCAY

RHONE

PO Venice

Lourdes

Ferrara

ADR.

Florence

Madrid

SPAIN

CORSICA

ITALY

Rome

BALEARIC
ISLANDS

SARDINIA

Algiers

Tunis

SICILY

M

ALGERIA

— LEGEND —
Scale of Miles

TUNISIA

Tripoli

Sites of previous Ecumenical
Councils are encircled —

WHAT IS AN ECUMENICAL COUNCIL?

A Catholic View

What Is an Ecumenical Council?

by THORALF T. THIELEN

The Newman Press • 1960 • Westminster, Maryland

Nihil obstat:
    EDWARD A. CERNY, S.S., D.D.
    Censor Librorum

Imprimatur:
    FRANCIS P. KEOUGH, D.D.
    Archbishop of Baltimore

June 16, 1960

The *Nihil obstat* and *Imprimatur* are official declarations that a book or pamphlet is free of doctrinal and moral error. No implication is contained therein that those who have granted the *Nihil obstat* and *Imprimatur* agree with the opinions expressed.

Dedication

To the Baptist who taught me how to tie my shoes. He
was one of the most charitable men I have known.

To the two Lutheran families who gave time and effort,
Martha-wise, in full measure, on the day of my
First Solemn High Mass. They were living the
neighborly love which Jesus taught in His Gospel.

To the Protestant couple in northern Sweden who opened
their hearts and hearth to a foreigner in need. I
was a stranger, and they took me in.

To the Greek Orthodox Deacon from Constantinople who
lived in an adjoining room at St. Louis des
Français, in Rome. Our casual chats of a decade
ago, comparing Church doctrine and discipline,
are ever a pleasant memory.

Foreword

The thoughts of these pages are addressed to men and women, boys and girls, of all nations, races, creeds—to anyone interested in Christianity and its doings, whether through hope—or curiosity—or even fear.

These chapters do not pretend to expand the scholarly frontiers of ecumenical ecclesiology. They do not propose to re-unravel all the knotted skeins of conciliar history. Their purpose is simply to provide a clear background upon which to project a sound understanding of a twentieth-century ecumenical council of the Catholic Church.

Most modern-day Christians, under the day-to-day pressure of earning a living and of rearing a family, tend to have interests which are multiplied many times beyond those of their forefathers. Legitimate interests they are, too, but all of them take time.

Today's Christian wants to know—has to know—many things, yet his twenty-four-hour day is no longer than that of his great-grandfather. Therefore, he wants to get to the heart of a matter quickly. He can think deeply, but he wants to do it fast—at a gulp, as he takes his morning coffee—because there is still so much more to be learned and done.

It is to this Pressured Modern that these ideas are directed: to the girl who operates the IBM machine eight hours a day, to her boss, and to his boss. This "background" is for farmers, manufacturers, and miners; for housewives, secretaries, and social workers; for engineers, scientists, and astronauts—for all who are interested in the better place that this world will be through a united, more Christ-like Christianity.

Since this is not a theological treatise, it seems advisable to limit the references almost exclusively to the identification of direct quotations. Most modern readers are happy when they are not forced to stumble over footnotes. "To cite for the sake of citing is pure ostentation, particularly in works of popularization." [1]

On the other hand, for the members of study clubs, perhaps, or of discussion groups, the references which are given, and the bibliography will provide a wealth of material for extremely profitable and interesting excursions.

* * *

The author wishes to take this opportunity to express his sincere gratitude to three individuals who read the entire manuscript. By their suggestions and emendations they greatly increased the clarity, correctness, and detailed exactness of the entire volume. They are Mr. Peter J. Thielen, the author's father; Mr. Frank E. Fortkamp, a senior collegian at the Pontifical College Josephinum; and Monsignor Leonard J. Fick, regent of the College Division and head of the Department of English of the Pontifical College Josephinum.

T.T.T.

Contents

Acknowledgments

The author wishes to thank the following publishers for permission to quote from their publications:

AMERICA PRESS, New York

Will Christians Come Together? by R. A. Graham, 1959.

THE BRUCE PUBLISHING COMPANY, Milwaukee

The Living Christ by John L. Murphy, 1952.

HARPER & BROTHERS, New York

The Catholic Approach to Protestantism by George A. Tavard, 1955.

LETOUZEY ET ANÉ, Paris

"Concile" by J. Forget. In Tome III of *Dictionnaire de Théologie Catholique,* 1938.

MISSION CHURCH PRESS, Roxbury, Mass.

Everyone's Madonna by S. McKenna, 1941.

MOUNT SAINT MARY'S SEMINARY, Emmitsburg, Md.

The Church of Christ by E. Sylvester Berry, 1955.

NEWMAN PRESS, Westminster, Md.

 Christ's Church by G. Van Noort. Translated and revised from the fifth Latin edition by J. J. Castelot and W. R. Murphy, 1957.

THE PONTIFICAL GREGORIAN UNIVERSITY, Rome

 De Ecclesia Christi by T. Zapelena. Two volumes, 1954.

SHEED AND WARD, New York

 The Holy Bible in the translation of Monsignor Ronald Knox, 1956.

THE WITNESS, Dubuque, Ia.

 Prayer for the Ecumenical Council by Pope John XXIII, 1960.

Introduction

Christianity is stirring, even more than usual! Among Protestants the Ecumenical Movement has been gathering momentum for decades. Millions have a sincere desire for unity. They believe that Christ intended His followers to be members of one Church, and they really want to get on with the job of making this a fact, not just a fancy theory.

In eastern Europe, in northeast Africa, in Near Asia, millions of people—sincere followers of Christ, too—have the same deep yearning. They read Christ's prayer for unity in tongues that are strange to Western ears. But the meaning of the agonized response it brings is the same as that which trembles on millions of Christian lips around the world: "How long, O Lord, how long?"

Roman Catholics also, especially in England,[1] Europe, and the Near East, have been gathering with

members of other faiths.[2] They have been discussing
the rifts in Christianity, and the need for healing them.
The meetings have been small, quiet, friendly. A solid
foundation of friendship has been laid, deep and
strong, cemented by mutual charity and open-hearted
sincerity.

In a few words, all around the globe the yearning
for Christian unity has noticeably deepened, especially
since the arrival of a fighting atheistic Communism on
the international scene.

Into this atmosphere of longing, Pope John XXIII
projected his intention of convoking an ecumenical
council to study, among other things, ways of achieving Christian unity. That one simple idea, as it issued
from the Vatican, quickened the pulse of the Christian
world. Across the face of six continents buckets of
printers' ink splashed the news: "An Ecumenical
Council!" Comments ranged from enthusiastic to
guarded. Almost no one was uninterested. And yet,
paradoxically, such a great interest would not have
been aroused if there had not been a widespread misunderstanding about the very meaning of the phrase
itself.

In Christianity today the word *ecumenical* has two
specific meanings: 1. that which represents and/or
binds the whole Church which is in communion with
the Holy See; 2. that which gives evidence of a longing
for and an awareness of the need to search for the full
unity which Christ intended that His Church should
have. The first meaning is Catholic in origin. The second is Protestant in origin. The first is present in the

phrase *ecumenical council* as used by Catholics. The second is present in the phrase *ecumenical movement,* as used by Protestants and adopted by Catholics.

When Pope John announced his intention to call an ecumenical council to study, among other things, ways to Christian unity, the phrase was used by the Pope in the first sense; but it was understood by Protestants in the second sense. As a result many Protestants thought that their Churches would be officially invited to the assembly. When through subsequent, more specific statements, it became evident that only Catholic bishops would be invited, there was a temptation to think that Pope John was backing away from an earlier position of broadmindedness because of pressure from some conservative ecclesiastical advisers. Actually, he was merely adhering to the age-old Catholic meaning of the phrase all the while. He had never intended anything else; but he did want to emphasize that the Catholic Church, in her council, while treating other matters also, was going to make a special effort—in keeping with her convictions about the nature, identity and unity of Christ's Church—to aid separated Christians in their sincere and earnest search for the unity which Christ intended.

Thus, in spite of the misunderstanding, the words of Dr. Charles Malik of Lebanon, representative to the United Nations, remain true: since "the urge to ecumenicity is genuine and universal today," this council could turn out to be "an historic event of the greatest magnitude;" it could be "greater than anything that has happened so far in this twentieth century, or indeed in many a long century past." To say the least, barring a nuclear war, the ecumenical council, in the next five years, will make thousands of news items. It will be an opportunity to witness a rare event, only the twenty-first of its kind in history. But those who do not know the rules, even though they may be interested in the outcome, are going to miss at least ninetenths of the meaning of the whole affair.

When a man sees a game of football, or soccer, or cricket, he gets more out of it if he knows the rules. Who is allowed to play? What is each player's job? What does the referee do? Are there coaches? What do they do? How did the game develop? Was it always organized this way? What kind of equipment is used? And last, but most important, *what are they doing* and *what are they trying to do?*

When people read about the ecumenical council— and they will, because they are interested in its purpose—they will get much more out of it, if they "know the rules." What is it, really? Who are the members? How did the councils develop? Where does the name come from? Who has the right to start one? Who presides? When is the whole affair really official? What is its authority? What is its value? Does *everybody* have to agree? How necessary is an ecumenical council? How many others have there been? Where? What did they do? What is this one trying to do?

There is a final question, too, which does not have a parallel for a non-player in a game of football or cricket: what can I do to help?

Strange though it seems at first, in the coming

council *everyone can help—and anyone!* No matter who he is, no matter what his creed or color, at the very least he can pray sincerely and earnestly to the Creator that all Christians may grow in virtue and in the love of God, and that they may recognize the real unity which Christ wants, the unity which everyone knows will make this a better planet to live on and, in a few years, to come back to.

It would be almost a diabolical mistake for anyone to think that his prayer would be only a small contribution, or ineffective, and that, therefore, its omission would make no difference. Any sincere prayer makes a divinely guaranteed difference. In a very real and personal way Christian unity depends on you and me. The united prayer of Christians sincerely begging God to show them the way to the unity He intends will be, in the last analysis, the most powerful aid that the council will have.

The long-range purpose of these pages is to stimulate and increase that aid. The desire to help can be stirred into action by knowing what an ecumenical council is. The will to pray can be set aglow by understanding what *this* one *hopes* to do and by having an intelligent grasp of what it actually *is* doing as the months go by.

WHAT IS AN ECUMENICAL COUNCIL?

CHAPTER I

The Ingredients of Unity

Difficulties standing in the way to Christian unity seem to be very great. Yet it is the belief of no less informed a person than Pope John XXIII that it "can be achieved, and be achieved with perfection," if everyone approaches the problem with charity and with a sincere continuing effort to understand, with a willingness to enter into discussions and to explore the possibilities. This does not mean that anyone should be prepared to give up truth; but it does mean that everyone should be prepared, no matter who he is, to grow in his understanding of the truth. Factual truth is a thing in itself, something which is outside the mind, something which does not depend on our intellectual approval for its existence. Five plus five equal ten. Whether I understand it or not, whether I express it correctly or not, whether others understand my statement about it or not: the

3

fact remains the same. But as soon as two parties are concerned, there are actually three steps which are involved before even those two can agree, before they can be united, on so simple a truth as this: five plus five equal ten.

First, both parties have to *understand* the truth itself correctly, e.g., they both have to understand the same amount by the words "five" and "ten." If not, they won't agree; there won't be unity. Secondly, both parties have to *express* the truth in a correct way. If not, there will be disagreement. They may both have the truth, but one or the other, or both, is not saying it properly. Third, each party has to *understand the other's* expression in the sense in which the speaker means it. If one hears the statement, "Five plus five are ten," he has to understand, before he can agree, that it means the same as when he himself says, "Five *with* five *equal* ten."

The proper expression of a truth is important; so is its comprehension by the hearer. Recall for an instant the fictional misunderstanding of an Eastener and his Midwestern friend as they walked along the banks of the Ohio one spring morning. Said the youngster from East of Jersey, "Gosh, it's a nice morning. Listen how pretty that boid's singin'." Responded his pal, "Man, that ain't no boid; that's a bird." Came the surprised reply, "Oh! Gosh, sure sounds like a boid to me!" Fictional, but illustrative! And one wonders if perhaps our heavenly Father doesn't see a parallel in at least some of the disagreements which exist in divided Christendom!

Beyond a doubt, truth is one thing. Understanding it correctly is another. Expressing the understanding is still another. And being correctly understood, while correctly understanding one's neighbor's expression, is yet a fourth consideration. In so simple a matter as five plus five equal ten the process of agreeing, of being united in judgment, is easy. But such a subject as the nature of the society which the Son of God founded, and the unity which He intended it to have, is a truth which is not nearly so simple to handle. In addition to the general problems outlined in the example above, there are other complications.

First of all, what Christ started is not something which had to be such as it is because of absolute necessity. Rather, it might have been a number of things; but, in actuality, it is only what Christ really chose to make it. So there is the initial problem of determining just what His intention was.

Secondly, the matter has been complicated by the multiple misunderstanding and uncharitableness of bygone centuries, which must now be cut through and forgotten—utterly! To attempt at this distance to fix the blame for the un-Christian finger-pointing and name-calling of the past is to doom present hopes for unity before they get off the ground. Someone once said that in the long run men learn from history only that men never learn from history. Now is the time to disprove that judgment on a grand scale by showing that Christians have learned the need for charity. History teaches it, screams for it, cries for it, pleads for it.

Pope John has expressed the idea in this fashion:

the ecumenical council will not be concerned with instituting a historical process to discover "who is right and who is wrong . . . we won't say anything else [but] 'let us reunite, let us end discussions.' . . . we shall tell them to let us stop quarrelling and get on together." And finally, in the same vein, he emphasized to a group of 2,200 Roman students: truth is important, "but it must be expressed without offending Christian charity."

A third matter is this: the completely unconscious offenses which will undoubtedly be caused by people who mean no offense whatsoever, who are trying to be charitable, but who unknowingly stumble on phrases, or terms, or express ideas which in the mind of their hearers—for no matter what the reason— carry overtones suggestive of intent to hurt. For example I was surprised one day when a Protestant friend of mine told me that Protestants like to be called Protestants, not non-Catholics. For some reason or other I had gotten the idea that by using the term "non-Catholics" in referring to my Protestant friends, I, a Catholic, was being less offensive to them. The very thing I was trying to avoid, I was causing!

Instances of a similar nature are bound to be multiplied over and over, not only in unofficial discussions that may surround the forthcoming council, but also in writings, in articles, in books, even in a book such as this. Some of the "offenses" will arise as the result of misconceptions which are much deeper than my difficulty was. Sometimes the background of history and of environment can form and shape the very outlook of an individual without his being responsible for it. As a result, he may make a statement and presume certain qualifications. Then when his qualifications are not included in the idea which his listener gets, he may "be offended."

Father Tavard, in his excellent little volume, presents the following example of just such a misunderstanding:

The Church, we are told, represents a return to the magic and demonic phase of the development of mankind. If we closely examine this, it refers to the Catholic conception of sacramental causality: a sacrament, according to Catholic theology, works, not *ex opere operantis,* but *ex opere operato* [i.e., literally, not *by the work of the worker,* but *by the work worked*].

I have long been nonplused by the fact that many Protestants consider the sacraments of the Catholic Church as magical devices, whereas the same sacraments given in the Orthodox Churches look to them like interesting elements of a venerable, if over-rated, world outlook. I now believe I have found why the same sacraments are thus differently judged according as they are given by a Catholic or by an Orthodox priest. Reading and listening to the theologian I have mentioned, I have noticed that he understands *non ex opere operantis* as meaning 'independently of the dispositions of faith of the man who receives the sacrament.' Now in Catholic doctrine it means 'independently of the holiness of the man who confers the sacrament.' We face here a mere Latin misreading transmitted by Protestant theologians from professor to student. Since, on the other hand, Orthodox theology does not use the Latin expression—simply because Latin is not its customary language—its doctrine is respected, while the same doctrine in its Latin formula is labeled 'magical.'

This nearly pure case . . . may be taken as a symbol of what immense misunderstanding has to be cleared up on many points where Protestant theology has forgotten its Catholic starting point. Misunderstanding, no need to add, works both ways; and this renders all the more difficult the hard though pressing task of untying so many intertwining threads.[1]

If, while trying to unravel such threads, either party allows himself even to think such a thought as "how stupid is this fellow anyway?"—only that much of a thought—the cause of Christian unity receives another wound!

Truth is important, but "it must be expressed without offending Christian charity." With these words Pope John was referring to the active aspect of a discussion: to speaker-charity. There is a passive side, too. Call it "listener-charity": if the truth should be expressed without charity, whether consciously or unconsciously, the listener must have such charity that he refuses to be discouraged by disappointments, refuses to be offended. If he is unable to do that, then he is falling short of St. Paul's idea:

Charity is patient, is kind; charity feels no envy; charity is never perverse or proud, never insolent; does not claim its rights, cannot be provoked, does not brood over an injury; takes no pleasure in wrongdoing, but rejoices at the victory of truth; sustains, believes, hopes, endures, to the last.[2]

A more accurate description of true charity will not be found. The passage is so very full of thought that it is worth many meditations. Notice particularly: charity is patient, is kind; charity is never proud, never insolent; does not claim its rights, does not brood over an injury; takes no pleasure in wrongdoing, but rejoices at the victory of truth; sustains, believes, hopes, endures, to the last.

Such is the charity which both speaker and listener, by turns, must have as they seek the actual unity which Christ intended. For the unity of all Christians will be born only of the truth, correctly understood, patiently studied, and charitably expressed. Or put in formula fashion: truth plus understanding plus patience plus charity equal unity of all Christians.

CHAPTER II

The Advantage of Talking

Written words are difficult things to handle. Some sentences, no matter how they are phrased, or broken up, or combined, never quite express what they say when spoken aloud.

Written words usually labor under a fundamental disadvantage: they are unaccompanied by tonal quality, expression, emphasis, gesture, modulation. No matter how skilled the author, his words often need interpretation. Why is it that some of the best works, e.g., *The Old Man and the Sea,* often provoke the greatest number of talks by book reviewers whose avowed purpose is to explain what the author meant? *Hamlet,* probably one of the greatest dramas of all time, will provoke interpretations and discussions on the precise nature of the fundamental flaw in Hamlet's character as long as civilized man is interested in tragedy. If only someone had thought to discuss it with the author! Then, at least, there would have been some possibility of resolving the problem. With a spoken exchange of words, it might have been cleared up in a matter of minutes. All of which points to this: since the problem of Christian unity deals with so many things, since there is so much that needs clarification, while the areas of possible misunderstanding are correspondingly vast, it is *necessary to get together and discuss the matters face to face.*

Fundamentally this preference for the spoken word is an old, old idea, dating back to the time of the Greeks. One might almost say that they had a kind of fear of the written word as opposed to what they called the "living," the spoken word. The reason was that the written word "has no power of adaptation; it speaks in one voice to all; it can not answer questions, meet objections, correct misunderstandings, or supplement its own omissions." [1]

What was true for the Greeks is still true for all Christians: statements, teachings, positions made in writing often need the clarification of the spoken word. Thus it is possible that someone may think, from the reading and studying which he has done, that the position of a particular division of Christendom on a given doctrine rules out all possibility of unity.

To some, for example, the Church's teaching on the nature of an ecumenical council is just such a doctrine. They say that it is too limited, too exclusive, and precludes the possibility of discussion. They object that it is a closed circle which they are not permitted to enter.

It is true, of course, that in the words of Pope John, "the council is to convoke in the first place all the bishops of the Church who are in communion with the Holy See." It cannot, therefore, include any *official* negotiations or discussions with individual bishops or groups of bishops who are not actually "in communion with the Holy See," i.e., who do not actually adhere to the beliefs, worship, and regulations (creed, cult, and code) of the Roman Pontiff.

Accordingly, no formal invitations can be sent to any bishops or Church leaders who are not "in communion with" the Roman Pontiff. Still, it is being widely publicized that any of them who would like to come will be warmly welcomed as distinguished visitors and observers. Then, even though they cannot participate in the official discussions, debates, and decisions, there will be many opportunities for unofficial, yet serious, meetings and gatherings to discuss the various aspects of belief, worship, and regulations with those who are official members of the council. In this way a "visiting observer" will be able to explain his view and perhaps aid in bringing about a mutual understanding.

He may be able, through the personal, unofficial discussion, to bring out a point of truth that had not been realized by others before. Too, he himself may recognize a point which had escaped him in the written words. All in all, nothing will be gained by boycotting the council. On the other hand, something good will be accomplished by "visiting and observing."

First, the very fact of being present will be a proof of charity. It will be a good example to other Christian groups who may have taken, in the past, a somewhat negative approach to the ecumenical endeavors of the Christian world.

Secondly, even a bare minimum of face-to-face discussion, if conducted charitably and in a positive fashion, i.e., by emphasizing the points of agreement, will have the beneficial effect of showing the participants that they are actually not nearly so widely separated on many points as they had thought. It may even be seen that in some instances the disagreeing factions have been simply stressing different aspects of the same truth.

Then, with first steps made, Christianity will be in a position to go on toward "a unity of perfection" which would be "an historic event of the greatest magnitude." Meanwhile, Christians around the world must watch and pray lest anyone enter into the temptation to be uncharitable.

CHAPTER III

The Variety and Nature of Councils

When the Catholic Church talks about one of her councils, she means a gathering of her rulers, a properly authorized gathering, of course—not just a "wildcat" group—for the purpose of discussing and deciding what is to be taught and what is to be done in the Church.

If the word *council* is used without any qualification, its meaning is rather indefinite. But, in any case, it will have to be either *particular* or *universal,* depending upon how much of the Church is represented.

1. PARTICULAR

There are four main types of particular councils. The *diocesan* council is a meeting of the bishop of a diocese with the priests. Usually such a gathering is called simply a "synod." A *provincial* council is made up of bishops of an ecclesiastical province, the arch-diocese. When the bishops of two or more archdioceses take part, the council is called either *regional,* or *plenary,* i.e., full. And a *national* council, naturally, has all the bishops of a particular nation represented. Since it speaks for and to the Church in that whole nation, it is sometimes called "plenary." [1]

Before the decisions and regulations of a national or plenary council can become binding on the whole Catholic Church in one nation or area, they have to be approved by the Pope. That is one of the big differ-ences between such a council and the meeting which the bishops of the United States usually have each autumn in Washington, D. C. In the Bishops' Meeting there is no intention of legislating upon any matters in such a way that all bishops and dioceses of the coun-try must conform. Mutual problems are discussed; recommendations are made; agreements are reached. But it is not the intention of the gathering to make de-cisions which are binding and obligatory for all. Each bishop would be completely within his rights to re-fuse to follow the ideas of the majority, except, of course, in a matter of defined doctrine.

2. UNIVERSAL

Not everyone makes a distinction between *general* and *ecumenical,* but it is a good idea to do so.

A *general* council is a gathering which represents the bishops of all the dioceses of the world. It be-comes, or is, *ecumenical* when it is approved by the

Pope. The Catholic Church holds that, in her councils, even if all the bishops should get together and decide something, yet if the Pope would not approve it, that unconfirmed proposition would not be a binding one. To borrow terms from civil government, the Pope has a veto power which is absolute. It cannot be over-ridden by a two-thirds majority, or even by a unani-mous vote of the assembled bishops.

Actually, there were a couple of instances in the life of the Church in which a large number of bishops got together, thought they were having an ecumenical council, and intended to legislate for the whole Church. But as it turned out, they were acting con-trary to the directions of the Pope, and failed to ob-tain his approval. That is what happened at a council held in Ephesus, on the western shore of modern Turkey, in 449. It could correctly be called *general,* but it is not one of the twenty councils which are com-monly termed *ecumenical.* In the eyes of the Church, it was just a general meeting of the bishops which, since it did not have the Pope's approval, was really nothing more than the action of a headless body.

A human body, when alive and functioning prop-erly, has a head which directs its actions. It has nerve centers of varying degrees of importance which aid in carrying out the directions for the proper life func-tions of the human person. To some extent, the nerve centers work independently, but still they are under the direction of the head. If not, the body is affected by convulsions, or may even suffer a chronic spastic condition. A general council which intends to be ecumenical but does not have the Pope's approval is an ecclesiastical spasm.

On the other hand, there are definite limitations to the comparison of the Church with a living human body. It would be incorrect, for instance, to conclude that the head of the Church, the Pope, cannot govern effectively and validly unless the "nerve centers" of the governing system, the bishops, "go along" with him. First of all, the Church does not have a physical body. And secondly, it is a "moral" person, not a human one. It is a society, a corporation, a group of human persons bound together by a common will and purpose. In a corporation the constitution, the nature of the society, and the way it is administered depend upon the intention of the founder, or founders. If he, or they, establish that the society is to be ruled by a governing board which is headed by a presiding officer with absolute directive and veto power, then any action on the part of the governing body, as a body, taken apart from his agreement, is of no value.

Such, says the Catholic Church, is her nature, as established by Christ. For that reason she holds that even though only a relatively small number of the bishops of the world attend a council, still, if their gathering and their decisions are approved by the Pope, i.e., by the head of the "governing board," then what they teach and regulate is binding upon the whole "moral person" of the Church.

CHAPTER IV

The Official Members

For a council to be ecumenical, all the residential bishops, that is, all who by their office have governing power in the Church, must be called, or convoked: the patriarchs, primates, archbishops, and bishops of dioceses from all around the world. It is they who, together with the head, govern the actions of the society, the moral person which is the Church. Titular bishops (coadjutors, auxiliaries, retired) do not *have* to be called, but it is proper to do so; and once present, they have a voice in the deliberation and voting along with the rest.

During the era of the first nine ecumenical councils, up to 1123, not all the bishops were invited directly. Rather, just the archbishops, or metropolitans, were called; and they were asked to bring along a group of the bishops from the various dioceses within the province. Each patriarch had to be present, or at least had to send some representative(s). As a matter of fact, for the first eight councils (up to 870), all of which were in the East, the patriarch of the West, the Pope, was usually represented only by two or three delegates, who were not always bishops.

Today it is the custom to call to the council all Cardinals (whether they are bishops or not); all abbots and other prelates who have special jurisdiction over a small separate territory of the Church, in such a way that they are not subject to the local bishop; and finally, all the Abbots-General of various monastery groups and the Superiors-General of religious Orders. These, along with the residential bishops, are members of the council in the strict sense. They not only take part in the discussions, but they are given the right to vote on doctrinal and disciplinary matters along with the bishops.

In the past, except for the Vatican Council (1869-1870), it was not uncommon to invite Catholic civil rulers in an honorary capacity. In the early centuries their presence was very practical: they protected the members of the gathering, and they saw to it, or tried to see to it, that the council itself proceeded in an orderly fashion. But, considering the changed world situation, it would be incongruous for any heads of state to be invited.

Some priests, of course, specialists in theology and canon law, will be asked to accompany their bishops; but they will be present only in an advisory role. They are not successors of the Apostles in the power to rule the Church, and therefore they are not members of the "governing board" headed by the Pope.

CHAPTER V

The Power of Convocation

A council is a *religious* meeting. The official members are rulers in the Church. Their purpose is to discuss and decide matters of a religious nature. In short, it is a *Church* meeting; and since the Pope is the head of the Church, he, and he alone, has the authority to call such a meeting.

For a Catholic the Pope is the successor of St. Peter. In being told to feed the flock of Christ,[1] and in being promised the complete power in the church which Christ was founding on earth,[2] Peter was given the job of taking charge of everyone: the faithful and the rest of the Apostles, too. Even though each of the Apostles was given power to bind and to loose, still each was, in principle, subject to St. Peter. As *Apostles* —witnesses of the Resurrection called especially by Christ and sent to preach His message—they were all equal to Peter. But as *pastors*—in ruling the flock—

they did not have full charge as Peter did. This is not to say that he was constantly sending out directives. It is probable that Peter only rarely, maybe not even rarely, exercised his power over the Apostles. He had the right to, but there was little need. Through the use of special gifts God aided and guided the infant Church to such a degree that the necessity of Peter's intervention, specifically as supreme pastor, must have been almost non-existent.

The residential, governing bishops in the dioceses of the Church are the successors to the Apostles. In the pastoral office of feeding Christ's flock, they bear the same relation to the Pope as the Apostles did to Peter. Each one governs his own diocese according to the right and power intended by Christ, independently of his neighboring bishop; and yet each is subject to the directives of the head of the pastoral group, the Pope. Thus it comes about that no one bishop has the power to tell his neighbor bishops around the globe to meet with him in council at a particular time and place in order to discuss some special problems that have come to his attention, problems which need concerted action on a world-wide basis. But, as the successor of the permanent office which was established by Christ and first given to Peter, the Pope does have that right, for his "pastoring" power is as wide as the Church.

Further, if no one bishop can call a council, it goes without saying that no temporal ruler has the right to do so. First of all, a civil leader, as a civil personality, can have no jurisdiction to call a religious meeting about religious matters. Secondly, no one civil ruler, or even several of them together, has jurisdiction which is co-extensive with the dioceses of the Church, spread as they are around the globe. Besides, to claim that a secular power has the right to call the bishops of the world into a religious meeting for religious purposes is to mix up the civil and spiritual spheres of society. It denies that Christ established His Church as an independent society, with the right to carry out its spiritual purposes without being a servant of the state.

And yet, when one looks at the history of the councils in the first thousand years after Christ, it is easy to see that the civil princes did call the bishops to many of the ecumenical councils. They seem to give evidence of having done so independently of any request by the Pope. They speak in their own right; they give commands. When they suspect that the bishops may not respond, they sometimes threaten punishment. As the reason for their actions they give divine inspiration, or the duty they have of looking after the peace of the realm. Yet they never say that they are acting for the Pope.

Finally, the bishops, councils, and sometimes the Popes themselves recognized the right of the emperor or the civil ruler to issue such calls. In the face of such actions, it seems strange to find definite indications that the Popes considered that *they* convoked these very same gatherings.

It would seem, at first glance, to be an open-and-shut case of conflicting evidence. On the one hand, the Popes maintained that they convoked the councils; on the other hand, the emperors acted as if they were sending out the call on their own initiative and in their own right.

But there is a third possibility: that each was exercising a different part of the over-all job of convening the council. For instance, it would have been possible for the civil ruler to look upon himself as providing for the physical presence of the bishops in one geographical place, while it was still the Head of the Church who "called the meeting to order," or gave the gathering the *official* character of an ecumenical council. If one looks at the historical situation in which the early councils were held, it becomes plain enough that such, in fact, was the case.

For the most part, the first councils were made up only of bishops of dioceses within the Roman Empire. Actually, there were some Gothic bishops (probably from the district of modern Bulgaria) present already at the Council of Nicaea, in 325; but at no time during the first 1000 years were bishops from outside the Empire present in anything but very small numbers.

After the year 650, when part of the Empire (North Africa, Egypt, Palestine, Syria) fell to the rising Arabian power, very few bishops in the fallen territories managed to get to the councils. In this situation it was natural for the emperor to think of a Church council as a meeting of the bishops of the Empire. From that point of view, it was a simple matter to conclude that at times it was his job to get them together to decide upon religious matters which were spilling over into civil life in such a way as to be disrupting the peace.

Another very powerful, and practical, consideration was this: an emperor had a much better chance of getting a positive response from a greater number of bishops. With his financial resources he could provide money for those who were not able to meet the expenses of travel and of prolonged living in a foreign country. With the external power of the state at his command, he was able to threaten to use a bit of it on the bishops who were too content at home to bestir themselves. At the same time, he was in a position to promise physical safety both on the journey and in the council city. And that was no small matter.

If an ecumenical council rates headlines in today's society of world councils and summit meetings, imagine what it must have meant in the early centuries to have bishops from all over the world converge upon one country and city. There were no newspapers, no television or movies to distract the attention of the populace of the council city from the religious discussions which were taking place. At times the excitement of the people reached fever pitch in an atmosphere that was already tense with the doctrinal disagreement for which the meeting had been called. All in all, attending a council did not present such pleasant physical circumstances of transportation and residence as the modern world takes for granted. Sometimes it was downright dangerous. Archbishop Flavian, the patriarch of Constantinople, eventually died of wounds received in a beating at Ephesus in

449, at the general council which was originally intended to be ecumenical, but which had all papal approval withdrawn.

Extreme violence was, of course, exceptional; but minor disturbances, inconveniences, and difficulties were common. The emperors were in the best position to keep the difficulties to a minimum. Accordingly, they sometimes took charge of assembling and protecting the bishops of the Church, that is, the "material" of a council. But they did not pretend to give a council its formal character and validity. They considered that the religious deliberations and decisions were the exclusive domain of the bishops. Thus, for instance, in sending one of his officers to Ephesus to maintain public order at the Council of 431, Theodosius II pointed out that only bishops were permitted to take part in the Church deliberations on doctrine, and that, therefore, he, the peace officer, as a layman, was forbidden to be a part of those discussions.[3] Some sixteen or seventeen years later, when calling the rulers of the Church to what turned out to be the Robber Council of 449, the same emperor again remarked that the care of religion and truth belonged completely to the bishops.[4]

Taking all of these considerations together, one can correctly say that only a Pope can convoke a council. And yet civil rulers did so too! Such a statement would, of course, be a contradiction except for the fact that the term *convocation* admits of different aspects.

The emperors sometimes gathered the "material" for the conciliar assemblies, but they did not intend or even pretend to invest them with power.[5] That came from the head of the Church, the Pope. It was papal authority which gave the councils their official standing.

And, in view of the circumstances of the times, it seems that the Popes were acting quite prudently. It would have been very difficult for them to overcome the great practical difficulties which stood in the way of achieving *material* convocation. They left that to the emperors; and they were satisfied to provide the official character, the *formal* convocation, which could come from them alone, either before, during, or even after the council.

CHAPTER VI

The Right
of Presiding

According to the present laws of the Church the Pope is in complete charge of a council. But does he *have* to be? Could he change the law and turn everything over to someone else, while he looked after the rest of the Church?

To see the picture properly, one must distinguish at least two, if not three, ways in which the office of presiding may be exercised: 1. formally, 2. protectively, 3. honorarily.

A formal presidency is one which actually directs a meeting, draws up the list of matters to be discussed, guides the deliberations, oversees the formulation of conclusions that are reached, and, in short, gives the meeting its official character while it is in session. The job of a protective presiding officer is easily understood. It is his task to provide a peaceful atmosphere for the gathering to work in: he is to protect the mem-

bers from one another (if need be) and from undue
outside pressure.

Finally, the idea of an honorary president is a familiar one. He may sign his name first on the official
roster, be presented first to visiting dignitaries, and
occupy a special place in processions and at the
banquet table, but his "presidency" gives him no
special legal rights or powers under the law.

From what has been already said, someone might
jump to the conclusion that the Popes were the ones
who formally presided at the councils, and the emperors were never more than honorary, or, at the
most, protective presidents. Such a statement ex-
presses enough of the truth to be allowed to pass, but
it does not tell everything.

To begin with, it is clear that the formal presidency
belongs only to the Head of the Church. Only the
proper authority in any society—as set up by its constitution—has the right to call a meeting of the legislative council or of the governing board. In the Church
that authority is found in the Pope because he is its
visible Head. It is for that reason that he alone can
give the formal call to all the rest of the bishops to
meet together for the purpose of discussing religious
matters. The flock has been entrusted to him. The rest
of the bishops have only parts of the flock to look
after. The same reason holds here. The Pope is not
relieved of his care of the whole flock and of his position as Head of the Church merely because of the fact
that he associates with himself others who also have
power to rule in the Church. It would not make sense

to say that he loses his position as chief visible shepherd once all the rest of the shepherds are gathered
together in one place, and have been formally convoked as a council. It is not necessary, however, for a
Pope to exercise this formal presiding in his own
person. If he wishes, he can do so through representatives to whom he gives instructions and directions. In
fact, not one of the first eight ecumenical councils was
personally directed by a Pope. To be very exact, it
should be stated this way: through their representatives the Popes presided at the first (Nicaea—325),
third (Ephesus—431), and fourth (Chalcedon—
451). They sent representatives to the sixth (Constantinople—680), the seventh (Nicaea—787), and
the eighth (Constantinople—870). But it is extremely
interesting to note that Pope Damasus had no legates
at the second (Constantinople—381); and at the fifth
(Constantinople—553), after having agreed with Emperor Justinian that a council would be a good idea,
Pope Vigilius *refused* to take part in it, *even though
he was in Constantinople at the time.*

Again, this seems to be a case of direct contradiction! It is said that the only one who can officially
preside at an ecumenical council so as to give it an
official character as a council is the Pope. Yet, opposed to that statement is the fact that Pope Vigilius
refused to join a council which is nonetheless the Fifth
Ecumenical Council. What about it?

The correct solution is not the charge of inconsist-
ency, but the application of a sensible qualification: in
order that a council be ecumenical *already while it is*

in progress, it must be presided over by the Pope or by his representatives. But *even after the sessions are over* a council can become ecumenical and universally binding merely by later papal approbation.

Of course, if the reason for the original absence of papal approval lies in the fact that the (proposed) decisions of the bishops actually conflict with the true faith or with correct morals, no Pope can ever give his formal agreement. The infallible guidance of the Spirit of Christ would prevent such a blunder. Christ promised that. But He never promised, nor did He intend, to make the visible Head of His Church superhuman. He did not intend, either, that the refusal of a Pope to act, even when requested by the bishops to do so, be implicitly an infallible condemnation of the bishops' proposal. In order to have an infallible condemnation, there must be a definite statement to that effect; the omission of approval is not enough.

Thus it can happen that the reason for the non-approval of a council (or a part of a council) is the result of misunderstanding, misinterpretation, misinformation, indisposition, or misguided prudence on the part of the head of the Church. In such an instance that very same council can become ecumenical later on if—but only if and when—a Pope gives his formal approval.[1] That is what happened to the decisions of the group of bishops whom the Emperor Justinian gathered at Constantinople in 553. Their resolutions were approved later, either by Pope Vigilius himself, or, if not by him, then certainly by Gregory I no later than 591.

It would be a distracting and unnecessary detail to try to determine exactly which of the two gave the formal approval first. But there is another point which ought to be noted: the fact that Emperor Justinian must have considered that he did not have the power to give the gathering and its decisions the formal character it needed in order to be binding. He considered an official approval by Vigilius so important that he went to great lengths, even to inflicting physical hardship on the Pope, to get him to consent. Such actions on the part of one of the most "episcopal" of emperors are an implicit indication that even he recognized the truth of the statement which the bishops of the Council of Chalcedon had sent to Pope Leo I a century earlier (451):

Through those whom you sent to take your place [Leo's representatives at the council] you govern the bishops in the way in which the head governs the members; the faithful emperors preside for the good order; as other Zorobabels they exhort to the dogmatic reconstruction of the Church which is like another Jerusalem.[2]

It would be hard to find a clearer description of the clean-cut distinction which was understood to exist between the formal presidency of the Pope and the protective presidency of the civil power in the person of the emperor.

*The Need
for Approval*

It is sometimes said that a council must be ecumenical in its convocation, its celebration, and its confirmation, meaning that it has to be formally called by the Pope, be officially presided over by him, and have specific approval from him. Understood in such a way, the statement is obviously not true. If it were, one would have to omit the Second Council of Constantinople in 553. It was not officially called into session by Pope Vigilius; and while it was in progress, he refused to take any part in it. Yet it is called ecumenical because it was confirmed later.

That historical fact tends to arouse a suspicion: is confirmation really necessary, or might that have been omitted too?

The second part of the question is easy: in this case (Constantinople—553) there had to be a confirmation because up to that time it was just a case of the body working without the agreement of the head.

The answer to the first part—is confirmation ever really necessary?—is not so simple. The word *confirmation* refers to an official act which gives such a force to the decisions of the council that they become binding on the whole Church. It is quite natural to think of it as an act which is performed after the formulation of the decrees to which it refers. In the more recent councils, those during the second thousand years of the Church, such has been the case. All have been confirmed by a Pope in a subsequent act by which he clearly intended to express his approval of the decisions reached.

But a difficulty arises when one goes back to the first millennium. In some instances there simply is not a record of a subsequent formal confirmation. Some scholars say that that is all there is to the case: the confirmation took place, but the records have been lost. Yet a detailed study of the facts which are still recorded does not seem to bear out that idea either, for in some cases the councils indicate that their decrees were binding and obligatory from the very time that they were published.

The solution seems to lie in a less strict notion of confirmation. Ordinarily, it is thought of as an action which is subsequent to the council, and expressly stated *after* the official sessions have ended. Still, there is no absolute necessity which demands that a council must be confirmed in such a *strict* sense. What it does need is the cooperating action of the Pope in such a way that it is clear that the decisions which have been reached are his too. That is not the same as saying that the approval or agreement of the chief visible shepherd must be given expressly *after* the council. There seems to be no reason why that cooperating agreement is not sufficiently indicated, for instance, when a council carries out the firm directions which a Pope gives to his legates *before* the council begins. The decisions arrived at are then automatically those of the head of the Church also. And the same is true of any conclusions which are reached while the Pope is actually presiding. Since they are ideas which the council proposes together with him, that very fact shows that they are his too. Of course, if he would *dis*agree with a decision of even a large majority, that would change the whole matter.

That is what happened at Ephesus in 449. Pope Leo I had given some very specific directions to his legates, but certain factions in the council would not even allow the message of the Pope to be read. After the approval of some false doctrine and the deposing of some faithful bishops, the gathering degenerated into a free-for-all in which the papal legates literally had to flee for their lives. Naturally, when Leo I learned the facts, he withdrew his approval completely. He would not agree to bind the sheep in the way that many of the subordinate shepherds of parts of the flock wished to do.

Two things, then, have to be considered: 1. the nature of the Church as established by its Founder; 2. the record of the way that that Church has actually

conducted itself in the councils which she considers
ecumenical. The conclusion is simply this: a confirmation—or the official and voluntary agreement of the
Pope—is necessary for ecumenicity; but it may be
present antecedently, or concurrently, or subsequently,
provided that, if given by the Pope's cooperation before or during the council, it be not withdrawn when
the Pope sees that what is actually being done is not
in agreement with his plans.

Such an explanation broadens the ordinary idea of
confirmation. On the one hand, however, it satisfies
the demands that the decisions of an ecumenical council be the action of the governing body and its head,
i.e., of the lesser shepherds and the chief visible shepherd; and, on the other hand, it does not demand
more than history shows was given.

To summarize, therefore: if the decisions of a
council go beyond the directions which were given to
it by its chief shepherd, the Pope, or if they are
reached without his cooperation and agreement, then
they must receive subsequent approbation (confirmation, in the strict sense of the term) before they have
such force as to be directives which all the sheep must
follow.

CHAPTER VIII

The Extent of Power

The authority of an ecumenical council is based upon the inner make-up of the religious organization which it represents. Therefore, to see what its power really is, it will be best to go back to the very beginnings of Christianity.

The Church arose as a social group. Its members joined together to do what Christ had commanded. The reason: they wanted to be saved, to have a happy eternity after their life on earth. Thus, they did not just happen to sprout—Topsy-like—into a Church. They followed the directions, first, of Christ, and then of His special disciples, the Apostles. Nor were the Apostles elected by a democratic vote. Rather, Christ chose them out of the whole group of His followers. He gave them special attention and instruction and finally, after His resurrection, sent them to carry His message to all nations. At the same time He promised that He himself would be with them, in the sense of effectively helping them to keep the message free from error. Also, He would help them thus until the end of time, something which He could say and promise only if they were to have successors to carry on their work.[1]

But that was not all. It is well known that as soon as there is a real division of power in an organization, it is weakened, in a certain sense; not that the sum total of the power is less, but rather that because of the foibles of human nature and the possibilities of discontent and disagreements, it becomes more difficult to actuate the power, to bring it to bear on present problems, and to make proper adjustments to changing circumstances. Incidentally, civil democracies recognize this very same weakness in their governmental structure. Thus they sometimes decide beforehand that, in a time of crisis, much more sweeping power should automatically be given to the chief executive, for the specific purpose of coping with the special problem swiftly and correctly. But at the same time, fearing abuses, a democracy provides for the revocation of the special power after the crisis is past.

Christ understood both sides of that human difficulty perfectly: on the one hand, the inherent weakness of democracy in time of crisis; on the other, the danger of abuse of power when it is concentrated in one person or even in a few. Yet He wanted to make His Church, even humanly speaking, as capable as possible of quick, concerted, unified, effective action.

1. STRENGTH FOR EMERGENCIES

As God, Jesus was able to look forward to the end of time. He could foresee all the problems His followers would have to face. Of course, there would not be any danger that the group would really flounder or collapse, if He would decide not to permit it. But there was the definite danger that there would be less efficiency, that some of His sheep in each of the centuries to follow would not reach eternal happiness as He wanted them to, unless His shepherds, those whom He intended to put in direct charge of His flock in the field of the world, would be able to act quickly in any emergency, so as to lead, guide, and guard the sheep on the correct path.

Christ had probably often watched the shepherds as they grazed their flocks on the Palestinian hills. His disciples, too, even though many of them were fishermen, were familiar with such pastoral scenes. Even today one would have to be literally blindfolded to travel the road from Bethlehem to Jerusalem, and on north through the hill country of Samaria, to Lake Galilee, without seeing at least several flocks of sheep with their shepherds. That is the way it had been, too, for centuries before Christ arrived on the scene.

Everybody in Palestine knew how each shepherd was in complete charge of his own flock. He took his sheep from one good pasture to another, led them to water, protected them, defended them against all harm. But when an attack came, he had to be able to act quickly and decisively. If there were several shepherds keeping their flocks together, one of them had to be in full charge of the general governing and protection of the whole flock in order to afford maximum effectiveness. If not, when an attack came, by the time all the shepherds agreed on what to do and got organized, the wolves destroyed many sheep which could have been saved.

The work of a shepherd was simply part of the natural store of knowledge of anybody who lived in Palestine in the days of Christ. For centuries, too, in their sacred books and in their ordinary language the Jews had spoken of God as their shepherd. They were his sheep. A king, too, was a shepherd—a pastor—and the people whom he ruled were his sheep. So it was the most natural thing in Israel when Christ began preaching the "kingdom of God"—the title by which He usually referred to His Church—it was the most natural thing in Israel to call Himself the Good Shepherd and to refer to those who accepted His teaching and commandments as His sheep. And since He did that regularly, it was just about the easiest thing in Palestine for the Apostles to comprehend what He meant when He told Peter, "Feed my lambs." When He repeated it, "Feed my lambs," they knew that He was in earnest. And then when it came a third time, after the manner of the Near-Easterners when they wished to indicate that something was absolutely definite and beyond all question—"Feed my sheep"—they knew that Christ was considering this transfer of the flock to Peter's care to be something of first-class importance, absolutely as final and binding as if done in writing under oath.

To an Eskimo who, thanks to some angelic transport, might have dropped out of the blue at that exact moment, the words would have been so much nonsense. The meaning might have gone over the head of a youngster who had never seen a sheep except in his first-grade reading book. But to the Apostles who had seen dozens of shepherds and sheepfolds and who were familiar with the true stories of attacks on the sheep by wolves and wild dogs—to them, the words made good sense.

They knew that the Master had been talking about returning to His Father, that He was planning some changes. They did not know just when, or how, or what; but they could see that, since His death and resurrection, He was making definite preparations for turning His kingdom, His flock, over to their immediate direction. Not that He was really going to be absent, because He promised to be with them. They did not understand all He was going to do, but the "shepherd-sheep" idea—that was simple. That they could understand easily from the life about them.

They would not have expressed the idea in the technical language we are accustomed to use today; but the idea itself, if one had asked them, would have been the same, because in the background of what they knew of life in Palestine and of Christ and His ways, there was only one idea they could have: the Good Shepherd, for some reason or other, whatever it was that He was going to do, was giving full and complete responsibility to one of their group, specifically to Peter, to provide for quick, decisive action in any emergency which might arise among the flock of His followers. They saw that he was to be the chief shepherd in the field, taking "the Owner's" place. They themselves were to work with him in directing the Sheepfold, in spreading the Kingdom. They were to preach, to teach, to baptize. They, too, had been given the power to bind and loose in the Kingdom. But the full burden was being put on Peter, in a special way, over and above them, and even including them. No matter how they would have said it, they knew that Christ's purpose was to provide a ruler, a universal pastor, who would be the chief visible shepherd in the pasture of the world, and who would give to the sheep of the Kingdom of Christ's Church, a firmness, a unity, a foundation which would make them, as a group, capable of standing up in the face of anything that the powers of evil might have to offer till the end of time.

Notice, by the way, that since Peter's position was to give unity, and since the Church would need unity to the end of time, Christ must have been thinking in terms of successors who would carry on when Peter should die. Or again, since Peter was to shepherd the whole flock of Christ as it would exist visibly in the world till the end of time, Christ must have intended that, when Peter should die, there would be others who would step into the office of chief visible shepherd to guide the flock. In this way Christ provided that His Church should be as strong and firm as would be humanly possible in meeting opposition. There was to be just one person at a time in complete charge, one after the other, till the end of the human race.

2. SAFEGUARDS AGAINST ABUSE

At first glance, it would seem that the Catholic Church must be misunderstanding something that Christ did, or said, or meant. How in the world could He have left His flock so wide open to the danger of abuse by putting such complete power in one office, to be wielded by just one person? Considering human beings as they are, would there not be a grave danger that someone would occupy that office who would abuse that absolute power, perhaps even make the office hereditarily appointive, and pass it on to another rascal of his own choosing?

Any thinking man knows that Christ could not allow such a thing to happen. Thus it is possible to conclude, in all sincerity, that He would not have given such complete power to one man as, for example, the Catholic Church claims for her head, the Pope.

But a Catholic sees that Christ took care of the problem in another way. First, the power which He gave did have limitations: it extended only to matters of a religious nature. In the second place, Christ promised His own effective assistance to guarantee the purity and propriety of the teachings and regulations which would be given in these religious matters. In other words, He provided that the one who should be the universal and chief visible shepherd would not make any mistakes when teaching and intending to obligate the whole flock on a matter of faith or morals. With such a limitation and guarantee, Christ did away with any real danger of an abuse of power. He did not rule out, of course, the possibility that some of the chief shepherds might turn out to be very undesirable individuals, personally and morally—but God does not force anyone to be personally holy. As private individuals, He left Peter and his successors just as fallible and "sin-able" as anyone else. He made them *infallible heads of the Church, not infallible men.* As a result, the sheep of Christ's flock in the Catholic Church are doubly happy when they have a chief shepherd who is prudent, wise, capable, holy. But even if he is not, they are still happy in knowing that, no matter how bad he may be personally, still, as visible head of the Church—because of Christ's guarantee— he will not lead them astray by forcing them to believe something which is false, or to do something which is evil.

To a Catholic the Pope is a compass: from him he gets his bearing on how to find his way "home." A man lost in a fog, if he has a finely fashioned compass, sparkling, bright, well-made, easy to carry, is happy. But even if it is only a small, rusty, battered instrument, he is still secure—so long as it is guaranteed to be trustworthy in showing directions. And he does not feel in the least that he has lost his liberty or that his compass is a dictator when it tells him, in spite of what he may think or feel to the contrary, that true north and the way home lies in the opposite direction. There is a standard rule among navigators which runs something like this, "Know your compass; understand how to read it; and then follow it *always*. It will be correct long, long after you have been tempted to think that it is all wrong. Just follow it. You will be glad you did when your home port comes into view." That is about the way a Catholic thinks about the Pope and heaven.

It all comes down to this: Christ really "went us one better" than what we expected. In a way, it seemed to be kind of a habit with Him. He more than fulfilled what the prophets foretold about Him, for instance. He went beyond all expectation in the Eucharist. After He himself had pointed out that no man could have greater love for his friend than to lay down his life for him, He went on to remain with us, to do more for us after His death by remaining with us in the Eucharist. So, too, He did much more than what we would have expected in setting up the organization of His Church. We would have thought that He would divide the power. But, no! To give His Church the greatest possible human efficiency, He put all responsibility in the hands of one; then to forestall any abuse, He "kept His own hand in," so to speak, by guaranteeing freedom from error in the only sphere in which He had given power—in the universal, religious shepherding of His flock. In short, He provided the most efficient system, while removing the evil it could give rise to: forcing people to believe falsehood or to perform evil.

3. Conciliar Authority and Effectiveness

The authority of an ecumenical council is, in the last analysis, based upon the original relationship between Peter and the rest of the Twelve; for their office of shepherding the flock has been handed on to successors, the Pastor of Rome and the bishops of all the world. All of them together have the full responsibility for looking after the flock of Christ. Their authority, then, is the highest and most solemn that exists in the Church. That is not to say that a council is above the chief shepherd; for, being its visible head, he has been given the care of the whole Church, the council included. But the authority of the council is not less than that of the head shepherd either, particularly since it must include his agreement or it is not acceptable.

But, now, is this not a useless duplication of effort? If the council cannot do anything more than its head can do alone, why bother getting the body together? If its decisions are no more binding than those of the chief shepherd all by himself, what is the use of a council at all? Why create such a fuss and bother for so many particular shepherds? Why not let "the main one" take care of it himself?

The point of the answer lies in this: to say that a council's decisions have no more binding *authority* than those of its head pastor all by himself is not the same as saying that they do not have more *effectiveness*. First of all, as far as the Church is concerned, that is, the sheep of the flock, just the very fact that a greater number of shepherds are involved in reaching the decision tends to make the members of the flock more receptive. Or, to transfer to legal terms, the larger the number and the higher the quality of the legislators, the greater is their combined prestige, and the greater will be the chance that the subjects will accept the laws and obey willingly.

Next, respecting the shepherds themselves, they are human too, as they are the first to admit. When they are all called together to discuss and deliberate with one another and with the universal shepherd on important matters of Church affairs, each one finds it easier to accept the decisions that are reached, for they are his too. Each has the opportunity to study all sides of the problem, to understand the reasons for statements which are proposed and actions which are taken. The view of each shepherd becomes much more universal than would be possible "back home," even if "home" is a whole country. Because of such factors, each bishop will naturally work more whole-heartedly, with greater fervor, prudence, and effort to carry out the decisions which he and his fellow shepherds have judged to be right and proper.

And there is an advantage for the Pope too. Christ has guaranteed that in teaching matters of faith and morals which are clearly intended as definite for all the sheep, the chief visible shepherd will not make a mistake. But Christ did not free him from the natural responsibility of using ordinary common sense, study, prudence, the seeking of good advice, just as anyone in such a responsible position should do. For any head of the Church to decide that during a given month he would spend the time between 2:00 and 2:30 p.m. each day in setting forth at least one new infallible doctrine, i.e., just to sit down and "turn one out," would not only be highly imprudent, but seriously wrong. Since it is something for which special divine assistance has been promised, the virtue of religion and simple common courtesy demand also a high decree of natural diligence and care.

As a matter of fact, no head of the Church has ever attempted a definition without proportionate study. Whenever any infallible pronouncement was made by a Pope,[2] very serious and prolonged study always preceded. For example, before Pius XII defined the doctrine of the Assumption of the Mother of God, a special investigation was made of the theological implications involved. The statements of previous Popes and councils that might have touched upon the subject in any way were looked at very closely. What the writers of the early Church had to say, both in Eastern and Western Christendom, was checked in minute detail. And, most important, the Catholic bishops of the world were consulted. But there was no council. As a result, even though there was only one main question involved, it took comparatively much more time to make the investigation and to study all the replies.

When there are several matters to discuss, as Pope John indicated for the forthcoming gathering, and when the issues involved are so complicated as the subjects he proposed, the most sensible thing to do is to get all the shepherds together in one place. Such concentration of effort will produce speedier results which will be more zealously pursued by the shepherds themselves because they have helped in the formulation. Also, the directives will be more readily followed by the sheep because of the added splendor and prestige.

4. LAWMAKERS AND JUDGES

Does this mean, then, that the particular shepherds whom the universal pastor calls into council are simply his research workers, his consultors, his advisers? Bluntly put, are they primarily only glorified yes-men who add color and dignity to the pronouncements?

To put the answer just as bluntly: no! The supreme authority of the council is exercised by all the members, by all the shepherds together. All of them, each and any who have or are given the right to vote, do so as shepherds of Christ's flock, or, in legal terms, as judges and lawmakers. Some of the first words of the third session of the Council of the Vatican are these: ". . . the bishops of the whole world, being in session with us [the Pope] and judging. . . ." In plain words, *all* the bishops *judge!*

The same idea of rendering a judicial decision is contained in the discussion which took place before arriving at the final decisions of each session. The bishops, all of them, act in legislative and judicial capacities. If a doctrine is being defined, then each one who votes in favor of doing so is a "definer." As a matter of fact, in the Vatican Council each bishop used these words, "I, N.N. defining, have signed."

Even if the bishops in the course of their investigations and discussions come upon a defined doctrine which, under the circumstances, they wish to clarify, or restate, or only to re-promulgate in identical terms, still they do so as real judges. Of course, they do not doubt the truth of the doctrine while they re-study it, before presenting it again. That would be senseless because all reason for doubting is done away with by the fact that the teaching, when first defined, is guarded from all error by the divine assistance of infallibility. But it can make very good sense to re-sift the arguments, to re-study the evidence, to re-examine the whole matter for the purpose of giving their own confirmation and approval.

By such confirmative (as opposed to doubting) re-examination they may be able to express more clearly the concepts and reasons which lie behind a particular teaching. Or, because of a more profound understanding of Scripture, say, in the light of more advanced historical and archeological studies, they may provide clearer testimony for the acceptance of the doctrine. Or again, by using the knowledge of more recent historical discoveries and theological insights, they may shed greater light on the relation of the doctrine to other theological truths and to revelation as a whole. And finally, in examining the history which surrounded the formulation of the original definition, they may see more precisely, and thus be able to state more exactly, what was defined and what was not defined. For it is possible, particularly after centuries of time and many historical changes, for many members of the Church—though not the teaching Church itself—to misunderstand a specific point as it was originally intended by a council, just as it is possible for sheep to misunderstand exactly what it is that the shepherds want them to do.

In all such procedures, whether merely restating a doctrine or whether really defining it more specifically, the bishops of a council act as true judges. After all, the judge in any civil court does the same thing when he gives his official verdict on what the law is and how it applies to a specific matter. The fact that the law is already on the books and can be applied in only one way does not cause him to cease being a judge when he makes the only application possible. So neither do the bishops of a council cease to be judges when they examine and re-present an idea which has already been dealt with in a definitive manner by a previous Pope or council.

CHAPTER IX

The Conditions and Limitations

The Twenty-First Ecumenical Council will soon be swinging into action. Newspapers, with a view to catching eyes, will be tempted to banner headlines:

Council Defines Ways to Unity
Council Defines Change in Church Law

When that happens, what is the proper attitude to adopt? Is every statement a definition which must be accepted as infallible truth?

Quite simply, no! But that still leaves a problem: just what is infallible? How can one tell what statements contain absolute truth? In a general sense, "infallible" means free from error. But how is one to know what statements of a council are definitely free from error?

For a really satisfactory view, it will be best to con-

sider once more the help which Christ promised to the
group of Apostolic shepherds whom He put in charge
of His flock. What is the nature of the assistance which
He promised? What is its purpose? Are there some
conditions to be fulfilled before it is certain that the
help is present?

It will be recalled that before His death, when the
Master was speaking to His disciples about going to
His Father, He told them that He would send

another to befriend you, one who is to dwell continually
with you forever. It is the truth-giving Spirit; . . . he will
be continually at your side, nay, he will be in you.[1]

I have still much to say to you, but it is beyond your
reach as yet. It will be for him, the truth-giving Spirit,
when he comes, to guide you into all truth.[2]

And, as if the foregoing were not enough, after His
resurrection, before demonstrating His visible depar-
ture from among them by ascending from Mt. Olivet,
the Good Shepherd promised His own help to the
Eleven, and to their successors, in carrying out the
world-wide, all-time job He was giving them. Matthew
recalled for the early Christians that it happened this
way:

All authority in heaven and on earth, he said, has been
given to me; you, therefore, must go out, making disciples
of all nations, and baptizing them in the name of the
Father, and of the Son, and of the Holy Ghost, teaching
them to observe all the commandments which I have
given you. And behold I am with you all through the days
that are coming, until the consummation of the world.[3]

And Mark recalls that there was another idea, too:

Go out over the world, and preach the gospel to the whole of creation; he who believes and is baptized will be saved; he who refuses belief will be condemned.[4]

From words such as these—they were almost certainly not the only ones that Christ spoke on the subject—the Apostles knew that the Good Shepherd was promising them His help in their work of shepherding His flock. They understood that the purpose of the Master's promise to help was to guarantee their success. They knew from the Sacred Books of their forefathers that when God used the words, "I will be with you," immediately after giving a person a task to perform, it meant that that person would be successful in the work he was to do. For the Apostles, it was an indication that, in the work of teaching the Gospel, there would be freedom from error. For if, as official, obligating teachers, they could *possibly* make mistakes, the nations that were to be taught could not be expected to stake their salvation on the acceptance of teachings which might be wrong. In other words, the Apostles could never be really successful, unless people could be *certain* that what was being taught was absolutely correct. Therefore, when Christ promised His help for the success of their mission, He must have meant that *he was promising to steer them clear of all error in their official task of guiding the whole flock in the doctrine of His Gospel.*

But as always when God promised His help, it was naturally limited to the specific work which the person was given. Thus, the assistance promised to the Apostles and their successors had its limitations. First of all, they had to be teaching *as a group,* for Christ promised them the special assistance in that way, not as individuals. It was only in the case of Peter's supreme office that an individual was singled out.[5]

Secondly, they had to be preaching *Christ's Gospel,* for they were not being sent to do anything else.

Thirdly, they had to be preaching the Gospel in a *definitive* manner, intending it to be accepted by the sheep of the flock, the members of the Church. Such a presentation was naturally necessary or it would not have been proper to make eternal salvation hinge upon its acceptance or rejection. Yet that is what Christ did: "He who believes and is baptized will be saved; he who refuses belief will be condemned." [6] On the contrary, then, if they would speak as individuals, or if they would "sound off" on matters not strictly related to Christ's teaching and revelation, or if they would not intend their statement to be definitive, then they could not count on the Master's special help to keep them from making mistakes.

Finally, it meant that, even when speaking officially as a group, and about a teaching of Christ, or a necessarily related matter, they would have to *indicate clearly* just what it was that they were intending to teach definitely; for, again, it would be unjust to make salvation depend upon the acceptance of a proposition whose sense and extent have not been clearly indicated.

Briefly put, Christ promised effectual divine assistance to those who would be engaged in pastoring His flock "through all the days"—first to the Apostles, and then to their successors, the bishops and the Pope. But that aid is naturally restricted, so that there is a certainty of its guaranteeing presence only under limited circumstances. By checking to see whether all the limiting conditions are verified, the members of the flock can know whether a given conciliar statement of the shepherds is really guaranteed by the infallible assistance of Christ and of the Holy Spirit.

1. THE PASTORS MUST TEACH AS A GROUP

Except for the special case of Peter, Christ promised infallible help to the Apostles and to their successors only as a group.[7] Of course, in the case of a council this condition need hardly be mentioned. It is automatically verified because in the formal statements the bishops do speak as a group. On the other hand, the informal statements of individuals, or of preliminary discussions, do not enter into question, for they are not the pronouncements of the council.

2. THE MATTER OF THE STATEMENT MUST BE CLOSELY CONSIDERED

A. *Pronouncements which teach revealed truth* constitute the matter for which Chirst directly promised his "being with" the teaching group. If all the other conditions are fulfilled, these statements *are infallible*. Anyone who refuses to accept one of them is judged to be rejecting a truth which has been taught by God and is being officially proclaimed by the guiding shepherds whom He assists with His own infallible guidance.

B. Next, there are presentations of *non-revealed truths* which are so *closely connected* with something in revelation that a mistake in teaching the non-revealed truth would open up a real danger of teaching error about revelation. Because of the close relation, these matters *are* also guaranteed to be *infallible* and absolutely true. A person who denies such a proposition is rejecting a truth taught by God's officially established guiding shepherds, who are assisted by Him so as to be unfailingly correct in anything necessarily related to His revelation.

For example, if it had been possible for the shepherds of the Church to have been fallible in acknowledging Pius XII as legitimate Pope, there would be a danger of error in accepting as infallible his definitive teaching on the Assumption of the Virgin Mother of Christ. But, because of the necessary inter-dependence of the two ideas, the non-revealed truth that Pius XII was actually a legitimate Pope must also be absolutely true and guaranteed by Christ's promise of "being with" his Church. If such were not the case, the whole idea of papal infallibility would be simply words, and nothing more! That such, in turn, is not true, is known with certainty because of the infallible guidance which guarded the shepherds of the Vatican Council when, in union with the Pope, they defined papal infallibility.

C. *Explanatory remarks* give the reasons which lead a council to propose the various statements whose acceptance is being made obligatory for the whole flock. In one case such an explanation may present philosophical reasons. Again, there may be an interpretation of a passage in Scripture. Sometimes there can be the quotation of several biblical texts which, in themselves, as they stand, are expected to provide the explanation. But in all cases, unless there is a specific, clear, and definitive pronouncement of the council to the contrary, *explanatory reasons are not* to be looked upon as *infallible*. They are not necessarily free from all error. But, of course, that is a far cry from saying that they are therefore wrong. Since they have the backing of human learning and scholarship, one should not be led to reject any one of them as false, unless one has sound reasons to back up one's position. Even then, there is no reason to doubt—in fact, one may not doubt—the truth of the doctrine itself, for infallibility does not depend upon, nor was it promised for the protection of, the human reasons which are alleged. It is possible for an explanation of a council to be wrong, e.g., a Scripture text may be misinterpreted, but because of other reasons which the bishops may not have even realized, the truth which the council *thought* it was deducing from the passage still remains firmly true, since the council intended to teach a matter of faith or morals binding on all the faithful.

Neither the discussions which precede a dogmatic decree, nor the reasons alleged to prove and explain it, are to be accepted as infallibly true. Nothing but the actual decrees are of faith, and these only if they are intended as such.[8]

D. The *laws and regulations* which are set down by the council for the governing of Church life and discipline are *infallibly good, though not necessarily the best*. They are the fences and guardrails which are erected by the shepherds to make certain that the flock entrusted to them by Christ is properly guided along the paths of holiness to the "green pastures" of eternal beatitude.

Real sheep—the woolly kind—do not stop to worry about the safeguards taken in their behalf. So long as they get to the pasture, any pasture, they are happy. But an intelligent flock—as the human followers of Christ—are seeking a definite pasture. They want correct directions. They are understandably critical of the fences and guardrails, of the signposts and directions which are set up for them along the way. As they move along, they want to be as certain as possible that they are being taken in the right direction.

Christ's promise to be present with the Apostles and their successors, in order to make them successful in their task of guiding the flock, affords the desired reassurance. Because of that promise, the sheep, i.e., the members of the Church, can be certain that the fences and signposts, i.e., the regulations and the laws which the shepherds set up for all to follow, are definitely good, though not necessarily the best. They will, at the very least, aid, rather than detract from, the purpose of helping the whole flock along the way to "the eternal green pastures," and the enjoyment of the rule of the Good Shepherd face-to-face.

3. THE INTENTION MUST BE DEFINITIVE

For any formal pronouncements of the council to be infallible—no matter what the subject-matter of the statements—it must be made clear in some way or other that the bishops are intending to teach: 1. in their capacity as shepherds of the whole Church, 2. in such a way as to make the acceptance of the teaching a matter of obligation on all.

For this purpose no set formula is necessary; it is sufficient to mention the doctrine as *an article of faith, a dogma of faith, a doctrine always believed in the Church,* or *a doctrine handed down by the Fathers.* Anathema [a solemn denunciation] pronounced against those who deny a doctrine is also sufficient evidence of a dogmatic definition.[9]

Anything less than a definitive decree would be a matter for which Christ did not promise His assistance, because He gave it with a view to providing certainty in matters which would be proposed as obligatory, that is, for matters of life and death, salvation-wise, not for less important things about which one could hold wrong views and still reach salvation.

4. THE MEANING AND EXTENT OF THE FORMAL STATEMENT MUST BE CLEARLY INDICATED

This requirement is just common sense. It is not enough for the episcopal shepherds merely to have the intention to bind everyone to believe or to do something. They have to state clearly what it is that is to be believed, or what it is that is to be done.

Since Christ is divine, He is outstandingly fair and reasonable. It is unreasonable to bind anyone to do something, and to condemn him for not doing it, unless he has been told clearly what it is that he is expected to do. In other words, as the lawyers say it: a doubtful law does not bind. Thus, since Christ promised His assistance only for binding statements, a proposition which is so unclear as to be really doubtful in meaning is neither binding nor infallible.

CHAPTER X

The Spirit of
the Good Shepherd

When one is mindful of all the limiting conditions, it is easy to see that infallibility, properly understood, is not a menace at all, nor is it a restriction of legitimate freedom. Rather, it is the gift of a loving God. It is a powerful assistance which, by its very nature, and by its natural limitations, is guaranteed against any misuse.

Certainly, it is possible for people to misunderstand its nature. It is possible for those who are misinformed to be fearful of what they *think* it is. Even members of the flock may at times not notice that not all of the conditions have been fulfilled, and so may think that a statement is infallibly free from all error when actually it is not. But such misunderstandings are not the fault of God's infallible help. They are simply the result of a mistaken understanding of what His infallible help really is, and does. The existence of such misconceptions does not validly argue against the possibility of God's having given such a gift.

In fact, if one goes just a step farther and considers the point of view of the Good Shepherd Himself, a promise of infallibility seems not only possible, but even probable. After the providential preparation of the Old Testament, after all the humiliation and suffering inherent in the life and work of the God-Man who was the Founder and still is "the Proprietor and Owner" of the flock, after all the instruction and painstaking efforts which He went through to "get His Gospel across" to mankind originally, should it seem to be anything less than reasonable that He should take measures to see to it that it would be handed on in such a manner that mankind, His flock, would be definitely certain that it was *His* Gospel? How could He do that in a more *natural* way than by promising His effective guarding assistance to man's *natural* method of handing on knowledge? That He should do it in such a natural way—without the flare of private special guidance for each individual—fits in with the whole character of His dealing with mankind, for God does not want service out of awe, but out of love.

Recall the sacred history of special divine intervention in human affairs. How did Christ come into the world? In a blaze of glory? No, he arrived in a natural way, as a lovable baby. Just a sufficient number of people were made aware of the facts that it might be really proved and publicly attested that here was someone who was much more than human.

Was Christ rich, or his parents? No, as most people

of his country, his family had moderate means; that is, they were neither spectacularly rich, nor poor, in comparison with the standard of the times.

It is true that Christ worked miracles. The very word means wonders. But notice the circumstances. There was always the rectification of a wrong of some type. There was always the intention to aid, never the intention to perform merely to impress. Thus, for example, when Herod desired "signs," Christ refused to oblige with "a wonder" merely for its own sake. On the other hand, when He did aid miraculously, if it was something that could be done partially in a natural manner, under the circumstances, that was the way He did it. There were just enough witnesses that it could be proved publicly as having really happened. For example, when He changed water to wine at Cana, who knew about it, who knew how it took place? Only the servants who drew it. Even the chief steward had to take their word for it, if he wanted to know the true origin. And the guests, too, could know its true origin only from the servants who drew wine out of the jars which they themselves had filled with only water. Christ could have over-awed everyone by making a production-scene out of it, but that would have been unnatural. It would have disturbed society more than was necessary.

All through the Gospel, from beginning to end, this is a principle which is followed: the Good Shepherd does nothing which is more out of the ordinary than necessary. In a way, it seems to be a kind of loving understanding that all good shepherds have: fast, sudden movements might frighten the flock, scare them, stampede them in the wrong direction, into doing the wrong thing. Why was it that time and again Christ cautioned: "Don't tell anyone, until . . ."? Or, on the other hand, why was it that so many of the Jews did not accept Christ and His miracles, if it was not that the Good Shepherd was so natural that many of them thought that they could explain all His actions—even His existence—without the supernatural? Still, the principle of being no farther beyond the natural than necessary was so important that He was satisfied to have His death appear to be that of a criminal, with just enough of the divine shining through to be easily noticeable to those who cared to look.

His very dying was really unnatural for Him. He was God. He could have kept His body vigorous and young indefinitely—to this day, and throughout all time to come—but that would have been unnecessarily unnatural. Instead, He chose to die, and yet to remain, by being really present in the Eucharist. Again, what is more natural than that He, as the food of the spirit, should be really present under the appearance of food, of bread and wine: two of the most natural foods of His homeland?

In a way, all through His life on earth the Good Shepherd "leaned over backwards" to get His sheep to follow without disturbing their natural way of acting anymore than was necessary. That He made use of human beings, all working together under a visible head, to form the Sheepfold of His Church, fits in very naturally with the social nature of all mankind.

Finally, that He should give infallible assistance to that Church, as a whole, and to the chief visible shepherd whom He appointed to take charge in the field, is in complete accord with mankind's natural method of handing on knowledge. A man does not grow in natural learning by individual infusion. He is educated by his forebears who hand it down to him. So, too, in His Sheepfold, the Good Shepherd simply sees to it that the religious forebears, the visible shepherds of each generation, never make a mistake when they hand on revelation. It is the spirit of the Good Shepherd who is always careful of the naturalness of the manner in which He moves, lest a sudden, extraordinary motion cause fear and trembling instead of love. Without doubt, it is one of the most subtle aspects of God's tender love for His creatures.

CHAPTER XI

*The Degree
of Agreement*

In Chapter III there is
the statement that the Church "holds that even though
only a relatively small number of the bishops of the
world attend the council, still, if . . . approved by the
Pope . . . what they teach and regulate is binding upon
the whole 'moral person' of the Church."

If that idea is taken together with the fact that at the
Eighth Ecumenical Council (Fourth Constantinople—
869-870) there were only 102 Eastern bishops, and at
the Eighteenth (Fifth Lateran—1512-1517) only 115
Western bishops, one is led rather logically to ask two
questions. First, how many bishops have to be present
at a council before they can be said to represent the
whole world? Second, of those who are present, what
percentage have to concur on a pronouncement?

To begin with the second question first. The
Founder of the Church, and of the group of Apostolic

shepherds who care for it, was ever a most reasonable
Person. Unless He gave at least some implicit directions to the contrary, He must have intended that the
group of shepherding rulers guide the flock and come
to decisions according to the ordinary reasonable way
in which any group of human beings decide on a
course of action: by majority rule.

To demand an absolute and mathematical agreement would be highly unrealistic. As a matter of fact,
too, hardly anything would ever have been settled by
a council, because almost always—if not absolutely
always—any given decree was opposed by one or two
or more of the officially voting members. To require
complete agreement of all the members would, quite
simply, make a council more of a nuisance than anything else; for it would succeed only in stirring up
more difficulties, unless, of course, one would consider
that such was its job in order to focus the attention of
the universal shepherd, the Pope, and to evoke his
infallible ultimatum. But that would be a ridiculous
rather than a reasonable procedure.

That a *morally* unanimous agreement should be
required also seems beyond reason. The term is am-
biguous and misleading. How great a percentage constitutes "moral unanimity"? Do 90% of the shepherds
have to agree on a particular decree? Or will, perhaps, 66 2/3% provide the required consensus? In
short, the term is so indefinite as to cause more problems than it resolves. It sounds learned, but it does
not say much.

It would be possible, of course, for the universal shepherd, the one who is given complete charge of the shepherding group by the Founding Good Shepherd, to decide that, e.g., "in the future 'moral unanimity' shall be required, and it shall be constituted by 75% of the voting members present." Such a requirement would be perfectly legitimate. As a matter of fact, during the Council of Trent (1545-1563), one of the Popes advised that no decrees should be made except when the bishops were in almost unanimous agreement. But that was a temporary directive of prudence which was given for the purpose of presenting a united front to the opposition of that period. It was not intended to be a standard principle for all future time. And in the absence of such a specific determination it is unreasonable to seek more than a simple majority.

It is the same with the councils as with all deliberating assemblies: the questions are validly decided by the majority of the members. To maintain the contrary is to will that the minority has more right than the majority.[1]

However, if the majority section would disagree with the Pope, then,

. . . granting such a possibility, I think one should reply as follows: the minority side in union with a Pope defining would have to prevail. And one further question could be asked: whether in such a case one was really discussing *conciliar* infallibility, or rather papal? But this question is of little practical importance.[2]

Practical, or no, it seems difficult to come to any other conclusion but that such a decree as that envisioned would not be conciliar, but simply papal.

Now, to the first question: how many bishops have to be present before they can be said to represent the whole group of the governing shepherds of the Church?

It is rather common to answer that what is needed is

a sufficient number from different parts of the world so that, morally speaking, they are judged to represent the entire episcopal college.[3]

Furthermore, Cardinal Bellarmine wrote that

the number cannot be defined accurately, but it should be sufficient to constitute a moral representation of the whole Church. There should be at least some bishops from the majority of provinces.[4]

Such an answer still seems to be unsatisfactory; it does not give any numbers; it does not tell how many parts of the Church must be represented; it fails to indicate how big a part may be represented by one person.

Perhaps a more satisfying solution can be had by beginning with a look at the term "representation" itself.

"Moral representation of the entire world" is usually thought of in terms of numbers and geography. Yet, in its root idea, representation depends on a more fundamental concept. The matter of numbers and locale is really incidental. After all, a nation of 175,-

000,000 Americans can be represented by 15,000,000 soldiers, or by only one diplomat. When the Secretary General is sent by the United Nations on a fact-finding trip to an area of discontent, he alone—one man —sometimes represents as many as a billion people.

These examples indicate at a glance that the idea of representation is not tied up directly with numbers and place of origin, but with the more fundamental concept of the right to act in the name of others. Therefore, to try to determine the exact number of bishops who have to be present in order to truly represent the group of shepherding bishops around the planet, our first job is to determine how, or in what way, any group of assembled bishops gets its right to act for the universal Church.

It will be recalled that no ecclesiastical shepherd, except Peter and his successors, has universal jurisdiction *in his own right* over the whole flock of Christ. In an ecumenical council he has it with the chief shepherd. It is only he, the Pope, who has the right to convoke such gatherings formally. When he does so, the conciliar bishops are universal judges, rulers, and teachers along with him. Therefore it would seem that those who do come, represent the whole episcopal college, regardless of how many, or how few, unless they be only a *very* few and from one isolated section of the earth. In such an instance the decrees would be papal rather than conciliar. But if there is a sufficient number present to call it "a gathering" in the ordinary sense, then they are in the official position of having the right to act in the name of the whole

Church. They have that position from the very fact that they answer the call of the universal shepherd (thus having his validating concurrence for universal jurisdiction), and have the intention of taking part in a gathering which is to decide matters for the whole flock of Christ.

Such a view, it seems—explaining moral representation primarily on the basis of papal concurrence and the intention of the council members—will answer the difficulties which somehow, otherwise—on the basis of numerical and geographical representation— never seem to get answered. Thus, quite frankly, it is hard to see how bishops from only the Greek East (as was the case in the Ecumenical Council held at Constantinople in 381) could even morally represent the whole Church, if *geographical* representation were essential. But the difficulty dissolves when one applies intent of the members, together with papal concurrence of approbation, as the standards of moral representation.

Of course, the whole question is really only a theoretical one as far as the more recent councils are concerned. For instance, the Council of Trent (1545-1563) had as low as 70 bishops present, but also as high as 252, in the last session. And at the Vatican, in 1870, there were 747 bishops, literally from all over the world.

What makes the question still more hypothetical, and renders a small council extremely unlikely in the foreseeable future, is the present specific law of the Church. If anyone of those who must be invited to the council cannot come because of a real hindrance, then he is to send a deputy and indicate what the difficulty is.[5] In other words, it is the general mind of the Church, as expressed in her law, that those who have participation in episcopal jurisdiction are to attend the council unless they have a just cause for being absent. In that case, they are to explain what the reason is. Such legislation makes the possibility of a really small ecumenical gathering extremely remote. And in the presently projected instance there is certain to be a large actual representation from all the world, except perhaps from the territories closed off by the Iron and Bamboo Curtains of Communism.

But that idea leads to a further problem: what about the bishops who are actually absent from the council and perhaps—though contrary to the law—do not even send a deputy? Does their agreement or disagreement have to be considered?

Briefly, no! They have been invited, and therefore when they do not, or even cannot, respond, they "are judged to yield their own right and to agree tacitly to all decrees which may be handed down." [6]

After all, once a majority decision of the shepherds has been approved by the universal shepherd, even the dissenting ones are expected to agree, because it is a decision which has been reached by those who have both the intention and power (when thus acting in union with the universal shepherd) to decide something for the universal flock. Besides, they have the infallible guidance of the Invisible Good Shepherd and of His Holy Spirit.

CHAPTER XII

The Degree of Necessity

As one considers the phenomenon of an ecumenical council, it becomes more and more evident how much the whole matter depends —explicitly, in modern legislation; implicitly, in ancient practice—on one individual, the Pope, the chief visible shepherd in the field which is Christ's Church on earth.

It is he who convokes the council. He presides over it either himself or through others. He has the final word when it comes to establishing the matter and method of the agenda. The Fathers of the council may propose additional questions, but they have to be approved previously by the one who is presiding.[1]

The Pope can transfer a council from one place to another. He can suspend it, or dissolve it. It is he who confirms the decrees.[2] No one who has the obligation of being at the council may leave until it is formally concluded, unless he has made known to the presiding prelate the reason for leaving earlier, and has obtained permission from him actually to depart.[3]

The decrees of the council do not have any binding power unless they are approved by the Pope and promulgated at his command.[4] If he should die during the council, it is automatically interrupted, and not to be continued until a successor in the office of universal shepherd gives the order to do so.[5] Finally, while the council of shepherds has supreme power over the flock of Christ in the Church, in no case does anyone have the right to appeal from the judgment of the universal shepherd to that of a council.[6]

Such are some of the ideas which are expressed in the explicit laws of the Church. From them, one can easily get the impression that an ecumenical council needs the Pope, but not vice versa. And, frankly, that is correct—again, with proper distinctions.

The chief pastor, or rather the Church herself, does need a group of shepherding bishops all around the planet—and out on the planets of the universe, if she should ever spread there along with the human race. It was the founding intention of the Good Shepherd that there should always be a group of guiding shepherds who would take care of His flock. But He gave no command that they *had to* meet in solemn session at specific intervals, or ever. Nor is there anything in the very nature of the Sheepfold, the Church, which He founded, which would demand such formal gatherings. In establishing the role of universal shepherd, Christ already provided a supreme authority which all by itself, because of His promise, has all the power and infallible guidance which is required to solve any problem, answer any question, or meet any difficulty. And so, *strictly speaking,* there is no need for an ecumenical council, in the sense of an absolute necessity, pure and simple.

But such meetings are—or can be—extremely useful. In a certain sense, one might say that they are *ideally* necessary: in order to achieve maximum effect, results which are as close to the ideal as possible, they cannot be dispensed with completely in the life of the Church. Juridically speaking, and absolutely, the Church could get along without them altogether, and still continue to carry out her Founder's mission. But because of the psychological make-up of the human sheep, the shepherds will do a more effective job of guiding them, if they plan together in face-to-face talks. According to Van Noort

Ecumenical councils are extremely useful because, (a) in an ecumenical council, where there are gathered together the lights of the entire Church, there are abundant means for investigating the tradition and mind of the Church and for laying down the disciplinary laws best suited to meet the necessities of the times; (b) the splendor of authority, native to the decrees of an ecumenical council, does a great deal to incline men to obey more easily; (c) decrees of reform, laid down in an ecumenical council are more smoothly and efficaciously put into practice; for it is quite connatural that the bishops should with greater zeal urge the fulfillment of those very decrees in whose formulation they themselves had a hand.[7]

Forget brings out the idea of necessity much more pointedly:

Universal assemblies, in certain circumstances, become indispensable for assuring effaciously the repression of errors or of abuses, and the triumph of right and truth. It can happen that, in fact, the legitimate authority and the sovereignty of the Pope is less well known, at least in a practical manner, and that it does not succeed in itself in realizing the doctrinal unity and discipline which is its proper object. . . . If, in such circumstances, the bishops of the whole world are called together to deliberate and to make enactments in common agreement with the Supreme Pastor, each one of them will accept them more easily, more graciously . . . with more wholehearted vigor and intent. Each one will apply them more wisely, will publish them, will carry them out, and will recommend them with more fervor. . . . If one thinks especially of disciplinary decrees, one can understand even better the important role, and, to a certain point, the necessity, which the bishops of the different countries play in their preparation and revision. After all, who should be better acquainted than they with the different needs of their dioceses, and with the abuses which should be eliminated? Who should know better than they the measures and the remedies which, when adapted to local temperament and usage, would have the best chance of bringing out an efficacious result? From all these points of view, sometimes a council appears to be not only the more appropriate means, but it seems almost to be the only appropriate way of pursuing a particular end; and in this sense one could say that the ecumenical councils are necessary with a relative necessity, a necessity which is not founded directly on the organic constitution of the Church but which results from the obligation which has been imposed upon the Church and which is imposed also upon the Pope, of taking in each case the best possible way of safeguarding the truth and of realizing what is good.[8]

Finally, there is one specific instance in which an ecumenical council was, psychologically speaking, a real necessity: in defining the doctrine of papal infallibility.

It is true that the Popes, at least since the time of Pope Damasus, in 380, had been speaking and acting in such a way as implicitly to teach their own infallibility, when speaking as heads of the Church, on matters of doctrine. It is also true that, in practice, the Church accepted such teaching as infallible. Yet, when it came to the point of explicitly defining papal infallibility, its extent and limitations, there was hesitation on the part of some, even downright refusal in the case of a few. Imagine what a furor would have been caused if the Pope had decided, by himself, to define infallibly his own infallibility! For defining *that* doctrine the ecumenical council was most certainly extremely useful and, to say the least, relatively necessary for ideal effectiveness.

CHAPTER XIII

The Beginnings

A learned treatise which intends to deal with a phenomenon from history usually starts with an account of the origin and gradual development of the subject to be discussed. According to that method, this chapter should have been placed at the beginning of this volume.

But the order of a "learned" work is one thing; the order by which human beings learn—with interest, anyway—is quite another. No one asks about the history of aviation unless he has become interested in it through his contact with aviation. A youngster is not really interested in the problem of where babies come from until, after a more or less direct and somewhat prolonged contact, he knows what a baby is. In the same way, this "background" has put off the question of where ecumenical councils come from until it has had time to see what they are.

But now the thought comes rather naturally: where *did* they come from? And what about the words themselves? For instance, who in the world thought up the outlandish term *ecumenical?* And, by the way, since the Greek councils call themselves *synods,* is there any difference?

The word *council* seems to come from the two Latin words *con* and *calare.* If that is true, its root meaning is *a calling together.* To the Greek mind, a meeting is what happens as a result of people being on roads which come together. For them, a gathering is a *synodos: syn*—together, and *odos*—road. But, for all practical purposes, the two words mean the same thing: a meeting, a gathering, an assembly for the purpose of discussing something. That is the way the early Christians used the terms.

In the writings of the first Church historians, the word *synodos* had already been incorporated into Latin, so that the two words were used almost interchangeably. Later, with the passing of time, the meeting places themselves, the churches and chapels, were sometimes called *concilia.* That usage died out, in turn; and gradually, in Christian speech, the word was limited to meetings of high officials—especially of the Church, but not excluding those of the state—when dealing with religious affairs. That situation lasted until the more-or-less amiable attitude of the civil rulers toward the Church disappeared. As a result, they themselves disappeared from the gatherings, and the word became limited, in Church usage, to a properly authorized gathering of Church rulers for the purpose of discussing and deciding what is to be done and what is to be taught in the Church.

As for the word *ecumenical,* it is anything but outlandish. In fact, its root meaning is just the opposite. *Oikos* is the word for *house* or *dwelling; oikein* means *to inhabit.* From that, the Greeks had the expression *oikoumene (ge)*—inhabited (land). At first, the term was used only with reference to Greek territory. Later, when Greek civilization spread east to the Himalayas, south to Egypt, and then, through incorporation in the Roman Empire, went as far west as Spain and north to Britain, the expression *oikoumene* came to mean simply *the inhabited earth,* the whole world. Accordingly, something which was of, or from, or represented, the whole world was *oikoumenikos*—ecumenical.

In the course of time, as a result of changing civil and religious circumstances, additional ideas became attached to the term *ecumenical.* Long before the Council of Nicaea, in 325, Roman citizens used the word to indicate something which represented the whole empire. To their way of thinking the empire and the civilized, inhabited world were co-extensive. After the Ecumenical Council of Nicaea Christians began using the term to designate things which either represented the whole Church of Christ, or were binding upon the whole Church. It was only after the schism of 1054 that Roman Catholics, because of their views on the identity of the true Church, restricted the use of the word to that which represents and/or binds the whole Church which is in communion with the Holy See.[1]

Turning to the origin of the gatherings themselves, it is easy to see that they began for two reasons: 1. it was the natural thing to do; 2. Christ Himself had given the Apostles a cue.

The Saviour had given to the Twelve the job of guiding His flock. He had given them the task as a group. He had promised that He would be with them to help. And they remembered, too, that He had even said that where two or three were gathered together, He would be in the midst of them. What could have been more natural than that in times of more than usual stress, when troubled by special problems, they should have gathered to discuss and deliberate together?

In the very first days after Pentecost, they met to choose someone to fill the vacancy which Judas created. Later, when more help was needed, they gathered to choose the first deacons. Still later, when the converts from Judaism began insisting that Gentile converts had to observe the Jewish ceremonial law of circumcision, it was perfectly natural for some of the Apostles to gather and discuss the matter, before coming to any definite decision. But while it was natural to meet thus, the members must have considered it something *more than merely* natural, for St. Luke reports that they published the decisions of the Council held at Jerusalem with the words: "It is the Holy Spirit's pleasure and ours that. . . ."[2]

It was the Apostles themselves, then, who initiated the practice of having councils. They were not divinely instituted, nor were they of purely human origin. Rather,

they are an *apostolical* institution; but the Apostles, when they instituted them, acted under the commission which they received from Christ.[3]

It might almost be said that it would have been unnatural if they did not have more councils than those mentioned in the Sacred Writings. But that, of course, would be only pure conjecture.

This, however, is known: local councils were not uncommon in the latter part of the 100's. There were meetings of the church officials of particular territories to deal with the rise of Montanism and with the Easter controversy. For instance, Bishop Apollinaris of Hierapolis states that

the faithful of Asia, at many times and in many places, came together to consult on the subject of Montanus and his followers; and these new doctrines were examined, and declared strange and impious.[4]

These councils would have been around the year 150. Those dealing with the Easter controversy were held more toward the end of the same century.

During the 200's such gatherings became more numerous, and by the beginning of the 300's they were rather common both in the East and in the West. Whenever a special problem arose, it was the accepted thing for the leaders of the churches which were involved to hold a meeting with the purpose of discussing and deciding on some concerted action or teaching.

In 313 the Edict of Milan, giving the Church its freedom, inaugurated a whole new situation. It was not that the Empire changed in its support of *a* religion. Rather, now, instead of supporting paganism, Emperor Constantine began to look upon himself as a special patron of the Church, the protector of the Christian faith, almost as a kind of civil bishop. The problems of Christianity became his problems too.

Arius injected his teaching into that context around the year 320. There were repercussions all through Christendom. Particularly in the East the bishops judged that the most natural way to handle the difficulty and to decide once for all what the true doctrine is, was to meet together in one great council. Emperor Constantine had the same idea; and since he had the material power and wealth to provide for their transportation and their living in a foreign country, he made the move to call them all together. That is the way the Church got to the First Ecumenical Council, held in the year 325, in the little town of Nicaea, in the northwest corner of modern Turkey.

CHAPTER XIV

The History in Brief

A history of ecumenical councils can vary in size from one summary page to several, complete, large-sized libraries. Both have their value.

This "background" is trying to keep the Pressured Modern in mind—the woman who has the psychological pressure of a business or of a home-making life at sea level, as well as the man who has the literal pressure of sealed cabins orbiting the earth at Mach 30. For both of them, and for all similarly tempered spirits, this synopsis may be in order.[1]

FIRST [2] ECUMENICAL COUNCIL

Place:

Nicea, the present-day village of Iznik in the northwest corner of Turkey, in Asia.

Year:

325.

Called by:
> Emperor Constantine I, 306-337.

Official Members:
> About 318 bishops, mostly from the East, though there were some few from Africa, Spain, and Italy. Besides, there were the papal representatives: Bishop Hosius, from Cordova, Spain, and the priests, Vitus and Vincentius, from Rome.

Held Under:
> Pope Sylvester I, 314-325.

Major Decisions:
> Against Arius (and Arianism), defined that the Word has the same substance as the Father, and that therefore the Son of God is just as divine as the Father. The Nicene Creed, which is recited in the Latin Rite Mass with a few variations, was formulated by this council.

Confirmed by:
> Pope Sylvester I, very probably; definitely acknowledged by many later Popes as being ecumenical.

SECOND ECUMENICAL COUNCIL

Place:
> Constantinople, modern Istanbul, a city in European Turkey, on the Straits of Bosporus.

Year:
> 381.

Called by:
> Emperor Theodosius I, 379-394.

Official Members:
> About 185 bishops from the East.

Held under:
> Pope Damasus, 367-384, but he had no represen-
> tative at the gathering.

Major Decisions:
> Against Macedonius (and Macedonianism), de-
> fined that the Holy Spirit is "adored with the
> Father and the Son."

Confirmed by:
> Pope Damasus, very probably; definitely by later
> Popes. It is important to note that only the Creed
> was confirmed. The disciplinary regulations—
> particularly a canon which began to give untra-
> ditional recognition to the See of Constantinople
> by claiming for it a primacy of honor after Rome
> —were not given papal approbation.

THIRD ECUMENICAL COUNCIL

Place:
> Ephesus: ruins of this ancient city can be found
> a few miles from the western shore of modern
> Turkey, some 35 miles south-southeast of Izmir,
> ancient Smyrna.

Year:
> 431.

Called by:
> Emperor Theodosius II, 408-450.

Official Members:
> About 250 Eastern bishops and the papal delegates.

Held under:
> Pope Celestine I, 423-432.

Major Decisions:
> Against Nestorius (and Nestorianism), taught that there is one person in Christ; against Pelagius (and Pelagianism), taught the necessity of the help of divine grace for the performance of works which merit salvation.

Confirmed by:
> The legates of Pope Celestine I and by his successor, Pope Sixtus III, 432-440.

FOURTH ECUMENICAL COUNCIL

Place:
> Chalcedon: the modern city of Kadiköy, a suburb of Istanbul, across the Straits of Bosporus, in the northwest corner of Turkey in Asia.

Year:
> 451.

Called by:
> Emperor Marcian, 450-457, and Empress Pulcheria.

Official Members:

About 600 bishops (all from the East, except a couple from North Africa) and the deputies of Pope Leo I, Bishops Paschasinus and Lucentius, the priest Bonifacius, and two others.

Held under:

Pope Leo I, 440-461.

Major Decisions:

Against Eutyches (and Monophysitism), defined the distinction of two natures in Christ, that is, that He has both a human and a divine nature.

Confirmed by:

Pope Leo I, except for the twenty-eighth canon which claimed for Constantinople a patriarchal jurisdiction which Pope Leo maintained was contrary to the previous councils and prejudicial to the traditional rights of the Apostolic Sees of Antioch and Alexandria.

FIFTH ECUMENICAL COUNCIL

Place:

Constantinople.

Year:

553.

Called by:

Emperor Justinian and Pope Vigilius. But the Pope withdrew his agreement before the council got under way, because of the manner in which Justinian was attempting to pressure it into enacting the decisions he desired.

Official Members:

About 165 bishops, all of whom were from the East, except for about a half-dozen from North Africa. There were no official papal representatives. The council became officially ecumenical only in its later confirmation.

Held under:

Pope Vigilius, 540-555, who refused to have anything to do with the council while it was in actual session.

Major Decisions:

Condemned some Nestorian-slanted writings which are usually referred to as the "Three Chapters."

Confirmed by:

Pope Vigilius, probably. There is question, however, whether his approval may not have been obtained under duress. In that case *his* confirmation was not valid. But it is quite clear that Pope Gregory I, 590-604, definitely accepted the council as ecumenical.

SIXTH ECUMENICAL COUNCIL

Place:

Constantinople.

Year:

    680.

Called by:

    Emperor Constantine IV, 668-685.

Official Members:

    About 175 bishops from the East together with the representatives of Pope Agatho: the priests, Theodore and George, and a deacon, John.

Held under:

    Pope Agatho, 678-682.

Major Decisions:

    Against the Monothelites, defined that the one person of Christ has both a human and a divine will.

Confirmed by:

    Legates of Pope Agatho and by his successor, Pope Leo II, 682-683.

SEVENTH ECUMENICAL COUNCIL

Place:

    Nicea.

Year:

    787.

Called by:

    Empress Irene and her son, Emperor Constantine VI, 780-801.

Official Members:
About 390 Eastern bishops plus at least two papal representatives, both of whom were named Peter: one, a priest; the other, an abbot.

Held under:
Pope Hadrian I, 772-795.

Major Decisions:
Against the Iconoclasts, defined the legitimacy of giving proper reverence—not worship, in the strict sense—to statues and to images of saints. Against Adoptionism, defined that Jesus is the Son of God by nature, not merely by adoption.

Confirmed by:
Pope Hadrian I.

EIGHTH ECUMENICAL COUNCIL

Place:
Constantinople.

Year:
869-870.

Called by:
Emperor Basil, 867-896.

Official Members:
Slightly over 100 Eastern Bishops in addition to the papal deputies, Bishops Donatus and Stephen, and the deacon, Marinus.

Held under:
> Pope Hadrian II, 867-872.

Major Decisions:
> The removal of Photius as the patriarch of Constantinople and the restatement of the true faith which was to be held by all. Also, there were decrees on the canonical method of choosing bishops, and on the right of the Church to be free from the interference of civil power.

Confirmed by:
> Pope Hadrian II.

NINTH ECUMENICAL COUNCIL

Place:
> Rome, in the Lateran Palace.

Year:
> 1123.

Called by:
> Pope Callistus II, 1118-1124.

Official Members:
> 300 Western bishops and some 600 abbots and prelates.

Held under:
> Pope Callistus II, who presided at the council himself.

Major Decisions:

The solemn confirmation of a concordat, an agreement, which had been formally drawn up between the Holy Roman Empire, under Henry V, 1106-1125, and the Pope. It ended the investiture conflict, a bitter quarrel which had arisen when the Church sought to do away with a long-standing custom which seemed to imply that civil rulers conferred the power of the episcopacy on a bishop by investing him with the signs of his office: the ring and the crosier. There were also many decrees aimed at the improvement of ecclesiastical life, particularly on the subject of clerical marriage and the appropriation of Church property.

Confirmed by:

Pope Callistus II.

TENTH ECUMENICAL COUNCIL

Place:

Rome, in the Lateran Palace.

Year:

1139.

Called by:

Pope Innocent II, 1130-1143.

Official Members:

About 1000 Western bishops and prelates.

Held under:

Pope Innocent II; directed by his legates.

Major Decisions:

Dealt with the papal schism that had begun in 1130 with Anacletus II, an anti-pope. Also legislated against such evils as usury, hereditary claims to Church property, and simony.

Confirmed by:

Pope Innocent II.

ELEVENTH ECUMENICAL COUNCIL

Place:

Rome, in the Lateran Palace.

Year:

1179.

Called by:

Pope Alexander III, 1159-1181.

Official Members:

Over 300 bishops plus almost 700 additional prelates.

Held under:

Pope Alexander III; directed by his legates.

Major Decisions:

In addition to the condemnation of the Cathari, a severely puritanical and anti-social heresy, and the decree that future popes would have to be elected by two-thirds of the Cardinals present, there were numerous decrees aimed at the reformation of the clergy.

Confirmed by:
Pope Alexander III.

TWELFTH ECUMENICAL COUNCIL

Place:
Rome, in the Lateran Palace.

Year:
1215.

Called by:
Pope Innocent III, 1198-1216.

Official Members:
412 Western bishops and some 900 additional abbots and prelates.

Held under:
Pope Innocent III; directed by his representatives.

Major Decisions:
Dealt with transubstantiation, papal primacy, heretical beliefs of the Cathari, the secrecy of confession, the holding of annual provincial councils, and the law of annual reception of Easter Communion. Among many other things, some arrangements were made for undertaking a new Crusade to the Holy Land.

Confirmed by:
> Pope Innocent III.

THIRTEENTH ECUMENICAL COUNCIL

Place:
> Lyons, in east-central France.

Year:
> 1245.

Called by:
> Pope Innocent IV, 1241-1254.

Official Members:
> Over 200 bishops plus many abbots and prelates.

Held under:
> Pope Innocent IV; directed by his legates.

Major Decisions:
> Deposed Emperor Frederick II of the Holy Roman Empire, who had been persecuting the Pope; levied taxes for the relief of the Holy Land. The red hats of the Cardinals date from a decree of this council.

Confirmed by:
> Pope Innocent IV.

FOURTEENTH ECUMENICAL COUNCIL

Place:
> Lyons.

Year:
   1274.

Called by:
   Pope Gregory X, 1271-1276.

Official Members:
   About 500 bishops plus more than 500 abbots
   and prelates.

Held under:
   Pope Gregory X; directed by his deputies.

Major Decisions:
   The Greek Church was reunited with the Latin.
   The procession of the Holy Spirit from both the
   Father and the Son was defined. Plans were made
   for a new Crusade, and there were several decrees
   endeavoring to bring about a moral reform.

Confirmed by:
   Pope Gregory X.

FIFTEENTH ECUMENICAL COUNCIL

Place:
   Vienne, in southeast France on the Rhone River.

Year:
   1311-1312.

Called by:
   Pope Clement V, 1305-1314.

is called

Official Members:

About 300 bishops.

Held under:

Pope Clement V; directed by his legates.

Major Decisions:

More taxes were decreed for a Crusade to the Holy Land (but the French king diverted the proceeds to his own domestic military coffers). The Knights Templar were suppressed. Several reform decrees were enacted, but their exact nature is unknown, for the official records of the council have disappeared.

Confirmed by:

Pope Clement V.

SIXTEENTH ECUMENICAL COUNCIL

Place:

Constance, a city on the northern shore of Lake Constance, between modern Germany, Switzerland, and Austria.

Year:

1414-1418.

Called by:

Emperor Sigismund, 1410-1437.

Official Members:

Some 30 Cardinals and about 180 bishops.

Held under:
> Pope Gregory XII, 1406-1417.
> Pope Martin V, 1417-1431.

Major Decisions:
> Dealt with the removal of papal schism, by inducing the three claimants to relinquish their position. Pope Martin V was then elected to succeed. There were numerous decrees dealing with false doctrine and with the correction of bad morals.

Confirmed by:
> Pope Martin V *only in part.*

> Some few deny that this council was ecumenical in any sense, but it seems clear enough that there were several sessions conducted under the presidency of Pope Martin V, the definitely legitimate pope who also gave his specific approval to all the decrees which had been reached by the whole council, as a council, i.e., when the bishops voted individually, and not according to national blocs, as they did for some matters during the course of their deliberations.

SEVENTEENTH ECUMENICAL COUNCIL

Place:
> Ferrara, southwest of Venice, near the Po River.
> Florence, about 150 miles northwest of Rome, on the Arno River.
> Rome, probably at the Lateran Palace.

Year:

     Ferrara: 1438.

     Florence: 1439-1443.

     Rome: 1443-1445.

Called by:

     Pope Eugene IV, 1431-1447.

Official Members:

     About 150 Western bishops; and, particularly while at Florence, about 700 Greek prelates, among whom were many bishops.

Held under:

     Pope Eugene IV; directed by him and by his legates.

Major Decisions:

     In July, 1439, an Act of Reunion between the Eastern and Western Churches was signed by 115 Latins and 33 Greeks. To some extent the movement to union on the part of the Eastern Church was motivated by the desire for united action with the West against the Turkish forces which were threatening the overthrow of the Eastern Empire. Besides, the Eastern leaders who agreed to the union were not wholeheartedly supported by the Eastern clergy and faithful. In 1472, nineteen years after Constantinople fell to the Turks (1453), Patriarch Gennadius rejected the union. The separation has continued uninterrupted ever since.

Confirmed by:
    Pope Eugene IV.

EIGHTEENTH ECUMENICAL COUNCIL

Place:
    Rome, in the Lateran Palace.

Year:
    1512-1517.

Called by:
    Pope Julius II, 1503-1513.

Official Members:
    115 Western bishops.

Held under:
    Pope Julius II and Pope Leo X, 1513-1521. They
    directed it through their legates.

Major Decisions:
    Decrees which, among many other things, dealt
    with Church reform, the relation between Pope
    and council, the establishment of a censorship
    over books, and the levying of a tax for war
    against the Turks.

Confirmed by:
    Pope Leo X.

NINETEENTH ECUMENICAL COUNCIL

Place:
Trent, the foothills of the Alps, in northeastern Italy, northeast of Milan.

Year:
1545-1563, with interruptions from 1549-1551 and 1552-1562.

Called by:
Pope Paul III, 1534-1549.

Official Members:
Varied from 70 to 250 Western bishops.

Held under:
Pope Paul III.
Pope Julius III, 1550-1555.
Pope Pius IV, 1559-1565.

Major Decisions:
First Period (1545-1549): on Scripture and Tradition; on the Vulgate translation; on the interpretation of Scripture; on original sin, justification, the sacraments.

Second Period (1551-1552): on sacraments, jurisdiction of bishops, discipline of the clergy.

Third Period (1562-1565): on Mass and Communion, the sacraments, purgatory, veneration of images, indulgences, discipline in the Church.

In view of the scope of the work, the difficulties under which its members labored, and the effects which were accomplished, this was probably the most outstanding of all the councils.

Confirmed by:
Pope Pius IV.

TWENTIETH ECUMENICAL COUNCIL

Place:
Rome, in the Vatican.

Year:
1869-1870.

Called by:
Pope Pius IX, 1864-1878.

Official Members:
774 bishops from all the continents.

Held under:
Pope Pius IX; directed by his legates.

Major Decisions:
On the Catholic Faith and on the nature of the Church; specifically also, the definition of papal infallibility.

Confirmed by:
Pope Pius IX.

This council was suspended in 1870, but was never officially terminated. However, Pope John

XXIII has implied in his statements that the council he is convoking is a new one, not just a continuation of that of the last century. It will probably be held in the Vatican and go down in history as the Second Vatican Council.

CHAPTER XV

The Three Threads There are, year-wise, two groups of councils, plus two. The first cluster of eight extends from 325 to 870. The longest span between any two was 127 years. But then, after 870, there was a gap of 253 years before Pope Callistus II convened the first one at the Lateran, in Rome, in 1123. It was the first of a series of eleven which extended down to 1563.

Another span of three complete centuries passed before Pius IX, in 1864, announced general plans for a new one which was eventually held at the Vatican in 1869-1870. Then, in 1959, at what might be called a standard interval in the conciliar life of the Church —some ninety years—Pope John XXIII indicated his intention of convoking still another.

The clustering of nineteen councils into two groups did not just happen. It was not mere coincidence.

There is a distinctly different thread which holds each of the two groups together. And there is a third thread since 1870.

The first eight councils were held—all of them—in the eastern part of the Church. Just the briefest survey of their activity (cf. pp. 91-112) indicates that they dealt chiefly with *doctrinal* matters. The second group of eleven—all in the west—was primarily interested in *reform* within the sheepfold itself, from the highest visible shepherd to the humblest sheep. This series ended with the great and multiple decrees of Trent. Now, with a projected council in the offing, as one looks back to 1870, one can discern a new thread which will unite the coming one with that of the past century and distinguish them from the preceding clusters. That new thread might be called *societal*. In other words, the past council and the one to come, by their doctrinal and disciplinary regulations, are interested in fostering a more united, active, lively Christian society, so that both mankind, as a whole, and each individual member of the human society will be able to advance—in and through the societal life of Christ's Church—to new levels of holiness and achievement.

The Church which the God-Man founded is not only a kingdom. It is not merely a sheepfold. Those "pictures" bring out certain aspects of the society; but they fail to emphasize a very important point: that the society, with its visible head and members, is really *living*. It is not simply a moral body, like a corporation, i.e., not simply an organization of human beings working together for a common purpose. It is that, but it is much more also.

First, in the Living Body which is the Church, the members are bound together, not only by the external tie of having the same goal, but also by an inner "life-principle" which directs and co-ordinates the actions of the whole Body, as it moves through space and time in the completion of its mission of bringing salvation to mankind. The "life-principle" is the special guiding presence of the Holy Spirit.

Secondly, this Living Body, which is called Mystical because of the special type of life which it has through the action of Christ and of the Holy Spirit, has Christ as its Head.

Briefly, then—and all of this is the inspired idea of St. Paul,[1] not just the concoction of the leisure hours of some theologian—the Church which Christ founded is a living body, strengthened and unified by the Holy Spirit, and having Christ as its invisible Head. It is the extension of Christ's presence among the creatures He personally redeemed. It is "Jesus Christ prolonged in space and time, and communicated to men."[2]

Like all living things, the Living Body of Christ, which is His Church, adapts to its surroundings. Ecumenical councils are reactions of that Body—under the guidance of Christ and of the Holy Spirit—when it finds itself in circumstances which in some way or other cause unusual difficulty for the continuance of its proper life activity.

During the first nine centuries of its life, the chief difficulty came from the activity of those who misunderstood the doctrines which had been entrusted to it for safekeeping. In the reactions which were the first eight councils, the doctrinal decrees—with the infallible assistance of the guiding Spirit of Christ—fended off the dangers. It must have been a difficult task, and a heart-rending one: making decisions to declare someone cut off from the Church, "the living Christ," because he was not adhering to the doctrine which had been handed down from Christ through the Apostles. Reading the long discussions of these gatherings, one gets the impression that it was a situation not too unlike that of a sorrowing man who decides that he must amputate his own hand in order to save the life of the whole body.

After the 800's, during the 900's, and on into the second millennium, there was a noticeable change in the life of Christ's Living Body. First of all, there was the terrible lesion of 1054, when the Eastern section declared itself independent of papal direction. To make matters still worse, the Life which continued in the West under the visible guidance of Peter's successor seemed to become sluggish, less active, less productive of the thriving, glowing holiness which was Christ's intent.

The reasons were legion. Here it is sufficient to recall the fact and to note that once again the Living Body reacted in defense. But this time the reaction was different because the nature of the impending evil had changed.

The emphasis shifted to that of reform, to re-toning the life of the whole Body. There were many such actions—ten, in all, between 1123 and 1517. Finally, in Christ's own permissive providence, it was only after violent upheavals of catastrophic proportions that the long and thorough-going Council of Trent (1545-1563) succeeded in putting into effect—still under the guiding assistance of the Spirit of Christ—the decrees and decisions which brought a re-surging of active life throughout the whole Body.

But that was back at the time when Spanish galleons were commanding the high seas, when conquistadors were carving empires in the Mexican highlands.

Three hundred years later, in the 1860's, the Church was still strong and active, still the self-same guardian of her Founder's Gospel, but the world had changed immensely. Not only new nations and new governments had come into existence, but a whole new secular and rationalistic outlook on life was growing up. It was strong, and it was destructive of faith in a Creator. The spirit of independence—well-intentioned though it may have been—which had lain behind the violent breaks of the 1500's, had opened the way, over the period of intervening centuries, to a spirit in which philosophy and reason took to rejecting a Creator and the idea that there should be any Church at all.

It was a spirit which, if left unchecked, was capable of jeopardizing the salvation of millions, and, ultimately, of mounting a frontal attack against the whole Living Body of the Church.

Once again it was time to react against a threat to the effectiveness of her mission. In the first ecumenical council to be held at the Vatican (1869-1870), the assembled shepherds set forth definitive truth about the nature of the society of the Church, about the nature of Catholic faith, and about papal infallibility.

Now, some ninety years later, though the world situation has not changed essentially, the evils have worsened and deepened. The philosophy of atheistic materialism, socialism, and Communism has succeeded in producing such a united, monolithic—albeit, fear-enforced—society that it constitutes a severe obstacle to the proper continuation and growth of the Living Church.

Effectively to oppose that united society of atheism, there must be a society which is united under God. And the unity must be not according to the whim of creatures, but in the manner which the Creator wills. Providentially, among divided Christians, there has been a renewed longing to find once again the oneness in Christ which they know they should have, and which they realize would make them more effective in overcoming the anti-God forces. With jet planes shrinking the earth, with rockets reaching into interplanetary space, and with a knowledge that only a *united,* God-serving society will be able to succeed against a menacing, atheistic socialism, the spirit of individualistic independence in Christian thinking has been melting away.

Christians want to be one. In so doing, they are following nature; for man is a social being, and needs social unity for proper life. Besides, they are following the express will of Christ who prayed "that they may all be one; that they too may be one in us. . . ." [3]

The new council, in giving special attention to ways for promoting Christian unity, will make use of this assuredly Christ-guided longing among Christians. At the same time, it will be giving evidence of the continuing active life of the Living Church which is the Mystical Body of Christ. Twenty times before she has "reacted to a threat" to her life—not that her life can be snuffed out before the human race is ended; but it can be seriously hampered in effecting good.

Because of the nature of the threat, the first eight reactions were mainly doctrinal. When the type of threat changed, so did the countering moves: they became chiefly reforming and disciplinary. And now that the attack has shifted so as to come from a united godless society, the Mystical Body is reacting by stressing, developing, clarifying, fostering a united Christian society. It will do this by a further examination and clarification of doctrine, by a modification and adaptation of better laws and regulations, by an investigation of ways to promote the more immediate advent of Christian unity. In short, those matters will receive prime attention in the coming council which will foster more efficient, concerted group action—the societal action of a united, active, living, Christian social body.

CHAPTER XVI

A Look to the Future

In an official statement published by the Vatican Secretariat of State, Pope John XXIII made known that the twenty-first meeting of all the shepherds of the Church was: 1. to provide for the edification of Christian people; 2. to be an invitation to separated communities to seek unity; 3. to modify the Code of Canon Law.

The purpose of the council, then, will not be simply to seek to find ways of promoting Christian unity. There are many other spheres of interest, both doctrinal and disciplinary, which will be studied, though, of course, all of them will be considered against the background of the aid which they can give in working toward the unity of Christendom.

I. SOME POSSIBLE PROJECTS

In general, anything which will make for a more living and lively, loving and lovable, Catholic social

121

body will also be a step toward achieving greater oneness with all separated Christians. Doctrinal decisions
which will provide for the edification—the building up
—of Christian people, disciplinary decrees which will
modify ecclesiastical law for dealing more effectively
with modern problems and world conditions—all of
them can indirectly be an aid to Christian unity.

But in the absence of any further official specifica-
tion of the agenda, it is quite impossible to determine
exactly what matters will be considered. At best, a
more or less educated guess can be made of what it
might do. What it will decide can, of course, be known
only after the decisions have been reached and published. After all, if they could be known beforehand,
little reason would remain for having the council.

Meanwhile, however, the human mind remains
curious. It wants to peer into the future. It knows it
cannot reach certainty, and still it wants to know:
what *might* the next council do?

The actual official agenda depends upon the decision of the universal shepherd. To assist him in arriving at a prudent list, he invites suggestions and plans
from committees which are appointed especially for
that purpose. Additional recommendations can be
made by other bishops who will be official members
of the council, but who have not been appointed to
the special preparing committees.

In the case of the Vatican Council, Cardinals who
were living in Rome were asked to present suggestions
on matters to be discussed. When the answers were
received, a special commission was appointed to study

them and to draw up a list of preliminary questions. At first the commission was limited to five Cardinals; later it was enlarged to include four more Cardinals, a secretary, and eight consultors.

Then, as the preparations continued still further, a predetermined number of bishops from both the Latin Rite and the Oriental Rites were asked about certain problems. At this point several more commissions were established, made up of theologians and canonists, who were to study the proposed questions thoroughly. Finally, the work of preparation was placed under the care of five special committees, each with a Cardinal at its head. There were eighty-eight consultors in all. The five committees were for: 1. dogma, 2. Church discipline, 3. Oriental-rite Churches and missions, 4. religious Orders, and 5. ecclesiastico-political problems.

It is quite probable that the preparation of the agenda of the coming council will be handled in much the same way. Still, for one who is interested in discerning beforehand what the council might do, a more important consideration is the fact that the episcopal shepherds, in proposing their suggestions, make use of —in addition to divine aid and grace—human judgments, advice, study, methods, procedures. It is these natural human elements which provide the would-be foreseer with the means from which he may be able to deduce some conjectures.

First, it is most natural to study the main problems which are facing the Church in its task of bringing Christ's Gospel to all nations. For instance, since one of the outstanding difficulties of the present age is the obstacle of a united, militant, atheistic society, it is natural to presume that, in general, the Fathers of the council will consider those matters which will tend to foster a united, active Christian society.

The second means—in addition to a study of express episcopal statements—is an examination of the thinking of experts in theology, in Canon Law, and in ecclesiastical regulations. In particular, it will be useful to observe the opinions of those experts who are already working in, and are actively acquainted with, the general fields indicated by the Holy Father.

Lastly, some idea can be obtained from looking at the example of the Vatican Council. It is true that some of the problems which that meeting was unable to consider—because of being interrupted by the national upheavals of the day, particularly by the invasion of Rome by the Piedmontese troops—have been provided for subsequently in the Code of Canon Law (published in 1917) and in papal encyclicals and directives. However, other problems still remain.

A lessening of marriage impediments, for instance, after the manner requested by the bishops of Quebec and Halifax, was incorporated, to some extent, in the Code of Canon Law; but it is possible that a restatement and even further reduction will be proposed by the coming council.

It is, then, on the basis of these three natural sources: 1. present-day obstacles, 2. the opinion of expert theologians, canonists, and exegetes, 3. some unfinished agenda of the Vatican Council, that it is possible to arrive at a general outline of matters which *might* receive the attention of the next council.[1] It will be helpful, merely for the sake of order, to group them under five general headings: 1. dogma; 2. Church discipline; 3. religious Orders; 4. the Church and society; 5. ways to unity.

1. DOGMA

A. There are not a few theologians who believe that some parts of the encyclical *Humani Generis*, written by Pius XII in 1950, may be reviewed and re-presented by the Council.

Among other things, there was a strong warning against many modern "isms." Existentialism, especially in its materialistic and atheistic origins, was condemned. Irenicism, the weakening of Catholic doctrine in an appeal to those outside the Church, was shown to be wrong. Dogmatic relativism was severely criticized. It maintains that expressions used in defined teaching are only relatively true, and so should be changed and accommodated to the changing ideas and vocabulary of modern philosophical systems. Also, Pius XII declared that it was in no way apparent how polygenism, according to which mankind is considered to have descended from more than one original human couple, could be in agreement with other defined doctrines of the teaching Church.

There are those who maintain that, in spite of the strong wording of the papal author, the encyclical was not received with the homage, respect, and obedience which was its due, and that its main ideas may, therefore, be re-stated by the council to achieve maximum effectiveness.

B. Many bishops and theological experts are of the opinion that the doctrine which maintains that the Blessed Virgin is the Mediatress of all graces is sufficiently clear to be proclaimed in solemn council. If such should be the case, there would still be a question of prudence. The doctrine appeals very strongly to the mentality of the Eastern Churches, but it might be greatly misunderstood by Protestant Christians. For that reason, it could, on the one hand, help to promote unity; on the other, it might lead to greater differences. In view of such circumstances the advisability of defining this doctrine at the present time will have to be studied very closely.

Incidentally, as understood by Catholics and by Christians of the Eastern Churches, the doctrine of Mary's mediating is not at all contrary to St. Paul's teaching that there is only one Mediator between God and men. Her mediation is completely subordinate to the mediation of her Son. It is only through Him that she can ask for and receive the graces which she distributes.[2]

C. In the face of the surging power of atheistic socialism and Communism, it is quite possible that their philosophical and theological errors will be more carefully and clearly re-presented to the Christian world, which will again be warned to stay clear of their temptations.

D. The value of miracles as a force in the personal

acceptance of revelation may be the object of yet another doctrinal investigation. It is known with definite certainty that miracles are a prime standard for judging when something is being attested by God. But the question arises: if they are such definite and sure standards, how can it be that so many people who seem to be sincere, can reject the evidence of miracles? In other words, the council may wish to set down a clearer, more specific teaching on the apologetic value of miracles.

E. In view of recent discussions, by both Catholics and Protestants, on the exact nature of faith, it may be found desirable to study more deeply the sources of revelation and to present a further clarification of just what an act of faith is, how it is made, what it is based on, and how it agrees with reason.

F. Finally, there is a chance that the council may desire to state more definitely the exact teaching value of papal encyclicals and of the ordinary teaching role of the papacy.

2. CHURCH DISCIPLINE

The field of ecclesiastical discipline and regulation is so vast, and the possibilities of change and adaptation so numerous, that only clear foreknowledge could indicate with any degree of real accuracy what the assembled shepherds—always under the guidance of the universal shepherd, and all with the aid of the Invisible Shepherd and His Holy Spirit—will judge to be in the best interest of the entire sheepfold and of the "other sheep"—the separated Christians—who are not of their fold.

As they gather from all the nations, the shepherds will have a universal view which it is impossible for anyone else to know. Consequently, their judgment may differ radically, and with good reason, from that of men who are not in their position and who do not have their divine guidance.

Keeping the fact of such limitations in mind, the following matters have been mentioned at various times by experts in Canon Law and in ecclesiastical discipline as being some of the things which the council may do in carrying out Pope John's intention of modifying Canon Law.

A. Modify some general legal concepts which have become somewhat outmoded. For example, the general laws which regulate the organization of a parish, in some aspects, seem to be considering a feudalistic society rather than the modern contractual system of living.

B. Incorporate into the wording of laws the authentic interpretations which have been made since the promulgation of the Code of Canon Law in 1917. There have been hundreds.

C. Incorporate recent laws pertaining to new secular institutes. These are societies whose members profess the evangelical counsels of poverty, chastity, and obedience, but live and work in the world, outside the cloister and common life.

D. Provide legislation to increase the role of laymen in the work of the apostolate, and to insure the continued proper growth of Catholic Action, "the participation of the laity in the apostolate of the hierarchy."

E. Relax and revise some of the ecclesiastical penalties which are demanded by the present system of censures for the infraction of various regulations.

F. Adapt the discipline which governs the activity of diocesan and religious clergy so as to place them in more favorable conditions for carrying on their apostolate.

G. Broaden the faculties of individual bishops to grant dispensations from present limitations and restrictions.

H. Provide laws for easing the problem of the unequal distribution of clergy among the dioceses of the world.

I. Establish practical means through which poor dioceses might receive aid from their richer neighbors.

J. Propose regulations looking toward the solution of problems which have arisen from the fact that in some countries the Church receives rather large sums of money for the support of the clergy and of its charitable and educational institutions in the form of revenue from Church-owned property and lands.

K. Investigate the validity of the contention that in certain areas of the world the Church could be more effective in its apostolate, if the dioceses were larger and less numerous.

L. Establish a system of greater centralization in the handling of marriage cases, so as to give them speedier and more concentrated attention.

M. As mentioned previously, re-study existing marriage impediments and, perhaps, make further adaptations.

N. Establish a special commission of experts who would prepare and publish an official Latin translation of the complete Bible from critically edited texts of the original languages. These are texts from which modern scholarship has removed, as accurately as it can, all copying mistakes, all additions, transpositions —anything which was not in the texts as they were written by the actual, original authors.

O. Consider especially three sections of the Church's discipline in which modern circumstances have made the observance of the law, in general, as it is stated, very difficult.

(1) *Servile work and Sunday rest.* Reasons of necessity, of recreation, and of custom, have become such that the law dealing with the prohibition of *servile* work on Sunday has become very difficult to interpret and to apply with any great degree of accuracy.[3]

(2) *Fast and abstinence.* The stress and tug of life in modern society has made the adjustment in the laws which regulate fasting and abstinence, as recently inaugurated in the United States, highly acceptable. It seems that the new regulations have actually increased the performance of penance rather than lessened it. It may be that the council will decree that the same discipline should be extended to the universal Church.

(3) *Forbidden books.* In view of the tremendous volume of books which roll off the presses of the

world (some 96,000 different volumes are currently available from United States publishers alone), there are those who believe that a revision and further refinement of the regulations dealing with forbidden books—and an easing of the manner of obtaining dispensations—may be a matter that will be studied and revised.

3. RELIGIOUS ORDERS

A. In some areas of present-day society the inability of cloistered communities to obtain the sheer necessities of life has moved the Church to allow some of their members to engage in work such as teaching. The income thus provided helps to support the whole community. It is thought that the council will very likely incorporate these regulations into the general laws for religious.

B. Some experts on Church discipline believe that the council may deem it wise to promulgate, as a law, a general reform of religious garb, along the lines which were so strongly advised by Pope Pius XII. Their thought is: 1. that religious garb had its origin in the modest clothing worn by the working class of the age and the land in which the religious group was founded; 2. that the original spirit of religious garb was to provide simple uniformity of dress, not unlike the laboring clothes of the common people of the era; 3. that religious garb, in not adopting modest modern styles, has lost the spirit of its origin and has, in many instances, become not only a protection against intrusions by the world, but a positive barrier which repels moderns from entering upon the religious life.

It is self-evident that, because of the emotional values which are involved, any obligatory change, or reform, has to be based on very prudent and mature judgment.

4. CHURCH AND SOCIETY

At the time of the Vatican Council, Bishop Spalding of Baltimore requested a review and clarification of the Church's teaching on her relation to the civil power of the State. Before it was suspended, the council was unable to give enough time to the subject. Since that time, various facets of ecclesiastico-political relationships have been treated by papal statement in encyclicals. But there are many aspects which still remain to be discussed:

A. There may be a further clarification of how and when a Catholic may co-operate with a Communist government.

B. Perhaps some of the Church's social teaching—the rights and duties of organized labor, the morality of "right to work" laws, the obligation of employer and employee to one another and to society—will be reviewed, detailed, and solemnly re-stated.

5. WAYS TO UNITY

Anyone who thinks that the coming council will succeed in ridding Christianity of all divisions, so that by the end of the century there will be simply the "one sheepfold" desired by the Invisible Shepherd, is quite obviously unrealistic. Religious convictions are a delicate and complicated subject in themselves. When they become ruffled and ensnarled by 500 to 1000 years of inherited disagreement and misunderstanding, the difficulty of resolving the entanglement—even in forty years—becomes so enormous as to be almost humanly impossible. In the case of unity among Christians, the very concept of the oneness which is desired is subject to interpretations which make even the beginning of discussions very difficult.

True unity, in the Catholic view, can be found only in the Catholic Church and in a return to that true Church by those who are separated from it by dogmatic error or by the absence of communion with the center of unity which is the See of Peter. . . . For the World Council of Churches, "unity" has a very specific meaning. The World Council starts from the assumption that unity is nowhere to be found among Christians and is something yet to be discovered. This organization has a tendency to seek for a "greatest common denominator," and to bury, so to speak, doctrinal differences under the cover of general agreement on a few "essential" tenets. By contrast, the Catholic Church believes herself already one in faith and destined by Christ to unite within herself today, as at Pentecost, the unity for which Christ prayed. For Catholics, Christ's promise of unity has been and is fulfilled in the Catholic Church. He who seeks unity, therefore, must go to her to find it. This conception, of course, the Protestants and Orthodox do not accept. But the WCC executive committee . . . conceded that progress toward unity called for a "full commitment on the part of each Church to the truth of the Gospel, to charity, and to a faithful interpretation of its deepest convictions." A Catholic's deepest conviction is that there is but one true Church and that where Peter is, there is the Church.[4]

In the face of such a fundamental difference, what an ecumenical council might be able to do to advance the cause of Christian unity is extremely hypothetical. The following possibilities are presented with that fact in view and are not intended to anticipate the judgment of the Church in any way.

A. If some Orthodox bishops should send official observers to the council, and if Protestant leaders should send representatives, there could be a decided increase in the friendly conversations leading toward a removal of misunderstandings. Such a development would be an augury of greater things yet to come, and would be a great step forward. Such conversations would aid the bishops of the Church in establishing a way in which to keep in permanent contact with the thinking and the advances of the Ecumenical Movement, while at the same time neither compromising nor watering down their own doctrinal convictions.

B. One of the biggest difficulties within the Church at the present time is an absence of men who are trained in the field of ecumenical theology. To ease this situation, the council may decide to make provisions for the development of such a corps of experts. They must necessarily be outstanding in their faith and loyalty, in their prudence and charity. It would be their task to work patiently and steadily toward filling the doctrinal chasms which keep Christianity divided. Even merely keeping them from becoming deeper would be a decided improvement!

A second aim of such a group of theologians would be to train a clergy which will in turn be effective in educating Catholic laymen to an attitude of sincere interest in, and sympathy for, the problems of separated Christians who are seeking unity.

C. The development of a "unity-minded" clergy would be achieved best, perhaps, by a deeper study of both Orthodox and Protestant theological positions and mentality. Of particular aid would be a detailed knowledge of the *reasons* which the various Churches adduce for their teaching on: (1) the nature of Christian unity; (2) the nature of the Church; (3) the relative value of Scripture and of Divine Tradition.

To achieve such an end—in the face of an already crowded curriculum—the council may decide that in the Catholic seminaries of the world, more attention should be devoted to the ideas of modern Protestant theology and spirituality as well as to the works of Eastern theologians (both ancient and modern).

Deeper study of the Greek Fathers would emphasize and clarify the elements which are possessed in common by the various separated groups, e.g., in Scripture, in Mariological doctrine, in the various bonds which still unite separated Christians with the true Church. On the other hand, a greater familiarity with Protestant thinking could show, e.g., that the doctrine of justification is in many instances no longer so widely separated from Catholic doctrine as is often presumed.

There is, of course, relative to Catholic teaching, a great deal of difference between the positions of the Orthodox and Protestant Churches in the field of doctrine. Catholics and Orthodox disagree on some points regarding the Immaculate Conception of the Blessed Virgin, the procession of the Holy Spirit in the Trinity, and the primacy of the Roman Bishop. But on such subjects as Scripture and Divine Tradition, Christ, the sacraments, the office of bishop, and the infallibility of the Church, the doctrine of the Orthodox is almost the same as that of Catholics, though it is often expressed in a more mystical fashion. Perhaps the biggest obstacles to unity, however, arise from the doctrine of papal infallibility, the question of divorce, and the placing of a Cardinal above a Patriarch, in the Latin-Rite Church.

The situation is considerably different in the case of most Protestant Churches. The disagreement with Catholic teaching is much more deep and extensive. Many do not accept the idea of an episcopal office in the Church. At the same time there may be a rejection of several sacraments, as held by the Catholic Church. Views on Scripture and Divine Tradition often differ radically. As long as such differences remain, the possibility of being united in doctrine with the Catholic Church is precluded. Much as she desires the unity of all Christians, the Church is convinced that she has the true doctrine taught by Christ. To be faithful to her deepest convictions, she must ever maintain that doctrine as it has been handed down to her. But that does not exclude a charitable and friendly discussion and restatement of the reasons for her convictions; nor does it rule out the possibility of a different approach which will be more adapted to the Protestant way of thinking, and yet guard unchanged the revealed doctrine received from the Apostles.

D. The council may propose again Pope Pius XII's teaching on the Mystical Body, together with a further clarification and analysis of the doctrine as it is contained in revelation. It is thought that a deeper study of the nature of the Church and of the relation of the Pope to the Church, especially under the aspect of the Mystical Body, might be a further aid to unity in that it might help to bring about a quicker meeting of the minds of Greek and Latin Christians on the subject of papal infallibility.

At the same time, such study—if pursued in the positive spirit of emphasizing points of agreement rather than points of separation—could lead to a deeper understanding of the fact, the manner, and the extent in which all Christians are even now connected with the true Church of Christ. Such knowledge would, in turn, be conducive to an atmosphere of charity and friendliness, a climate without which unity will never be achieved.

E. Finally, there are three special matters which the council *might* consider because of the effect they could have in producing a more vigorous societal life:

(1) A further increase of the laity in the corporate worship of the society. This would apply especially, of course, to the offering of the Mass. A development

of this type, together with a further understanding of the reality of the Mystical Body, might have the effect of producing such a glowing Catholic life that separated Christians would be naturally attracted to union with it. In addition, greater lay participation would be in complete accord with both Orthodox and Protestant manners of offering worship.

(2) *A more general use of the mother tongue of the people in their societal worship*—in the Mass, at Benediction of the Blessed Sacrament, Forty Hours' Devotion. The language of the people might stimulate more active and intelligent participation in the life of worship; and this, too, would be in agreement with the tastes of Orthodox and Protestant Christians. As such, it, too, would be an indirect aid to the cause of unity.

(3) *The inauguration of a married diaconate,* not only in one area, but throughout the Church. Such an institution would dovetail neatly with an increase of the participation of the laity in the apostolate of the hierarchy. Such men would be psychologically motivated—and would have the special grace of their sacramental office—to aid greatly in the spread of the faith in mission fields. They could staff religion courses in a Catholic educational system which is aimed at creating a laity that is educated not only in secular sciences but also, and equally as well, in the science of religion. Finally, the office could offer a reasonable solution for married Protestant clergymen who should wish to establish Christian unity with the Catholic Church.

II. THE FORMAL SESSIONS

The twenty-first ecumenical council, which is to be known as the Second Vatican Council after the place in which it is to be held, is to open formally on January 25, 1962, the feast of the Conversion of St. Paul, and the last of eight days of prayer which are devoted each year to begging God for the unity of Christendom.

Barring any extreme worsening of world conditions it is reasonable to assume that the official members in attendance will number over 1800.

The official language will certainly be Latin. A very great majority of the official members have been using it for years. It is the medium in which an exact and precise terminology has been developed over the course of centuries to express the theological concepts which are contained in, as well as based on, the revelation of Christianity. In fact, not to use Latin would open the door to confusion; for it is the one language which comes closest to satisfying the needs of each and all the members. If there should be any Eastern rite participants who may not be familiar enough with Latin to express themselves properly or to understand completely, ample provision for interpreters will be made. In short, the arrangements will be such that any official member will have the opportunity and the freedom to express his ideas clearly and to be understood by all.

One of the best ways to form a mental picture of a formal session is to compare it, in outline, with the

American-type political convention which nominates
a candidate for the presidency.[5]

As in a political convention the members are
numerous, a general program and order of discussion
have been previously prepared, many speeches can be
expected, and important matters are voted on publicly
by the whole assembly.

On the other hand, unlike the convention, every
member who wishes to speak is perfectly free to do so,
and may offer whatever suggestions, ideas, or motions
he thinks proper. At the Vatican council (1869-1870)
the members who opposed the views of the majority
stated clearly and emphatically that they were given
complete freedom and opportunity to express their
positions.

In a council session the manner of casting one's vote
is not varied. Whenever any issue is to be decided by
ballot, each bishop always votes individually, not as a
member of a particular region, bloc or nation. To use
convention language: the whole assembly is polled.

There is a vast difference in external decorum and
arrangement. At a political convention the seating
arrangement is orderly enough in the beginning; but
ultimately, in practice, it becomes rather haphazard
as individual delegates, in the excitement of continued
caucusing and balloting, leave their seats, stand on
them, take those of other delegates and lose their own.
Also, in a convention members of the press, radio, and
television usually enjoy, in theory at least, unlimited
access to all proceedings. At a council session the press
is not present, but a special liaison is maintained with

all news media in order to keep the world informed of the general progress and to prevent reporters from making guesses or starting rumors. So too, there can be no direct radio or television coverage except possibly for the solemn ceremonies of opening and closing sessions.

The arrangement of the place where the sessions are held follows a rather standard pattern. The Vatican Council can be used as a good example.

A temporary partition was erected to close off the right transept of St. Peter's from the rest of the basilica. (A transept is either arm of a church which is built in the form of a cross.) In the partition were doors which were often left open so that passing worshippers in St. Peter's could view the proceedings without entering.

The papal throne was at the opposite end of the transept, in the middle, against the wall. The 750 bishops who participated were seated on both sides, along the wall of the transept, on eight tiers of chairs. In the middle of the assembly, at a point within hearing distance of all, was the speaker's stand. Near the end of the transept, opposite the papal throne, close to the temporary partition, a balcony was erected to accommodate special visitors and observers, distinguished persons, members of royal families, heads of state and members of diplomatic missions in Rome.

Finally, in the external matter of clothing, a formal session of a council offers only contrast to a political convention. Each of the bishops wears a cope (according to the color of the vestments worn at Mass on

a given day) and each wears his episcopal mitre.
When the Pope, dressed in the distinctive robes of his
supreme office, adds his personal presence to the more
important sessions, the assembly becomes a body of
stateliness and grandeur which is seldom seen. In a
Catholic observer it produces a silent, reverential,
spine-tingling awe which is experienced nowhere else
on earth, for nowhere else is the splendor of God's
love and wisdom so visibly in act.

CHAPTER XVII

Prayer and Work

The final agenda of the Twenty-first Ecumenical Council may differ radically from the outline of possibilities which has been presented. In any given instance there may be many negative considerations which, in the judgment of the assembled Fathers, would outweigh the positive reasons for taking any step along lines which have been indicated.

The final decision on all matters is properly left to the wisdom of the shepherds of all the nations. A Catholic is able to do that without the least qualm of uneasiness. He knows that, following, as they do, in the office of the Apostles, who were sent to teach all the nations, they have an advantage which is one of God's greatest gifts of love: His unfailing help to do the job correctly. "Behold," He promised—God promised!— "I am with you all through the days that are coming, until the consummation of the world." [1]

What the proposed council will really achieve, what effect its decrees will actually have, can be judged only after the gathering has become history, some fifty years from now—or better, even, five hundred years hence —when the historians of the twenty-fifth century will be able to look back and make a more precise judgment in the light of now-still-to-come events. If, in the year 2600, they should be able to say even this much: "The Ecumenical Council convened by Pope John XXIII in the latter half of the 1900's was greatly instrumental in showing the way and smoothing the paths toward the union of all Christendom which we have enjoyed now during the past half century and which only recently has succeeded in overcoming the last vestige of atheistic Communism"—if they can say that in the year 2600, then the coming council will go down in history as a phenomenal world-uniting "event of the greatest magnitude."

There can be success, however, only if all Christians aid with their prayer and their work. There will be no unity in the one sheepfold of the Master unless there is a prior, sincere unity of prayer, by each Christian, for the sanctification of every individual who believes that Christ is God. Such prayer can be offered without an intercommunication of worship or of liturgical services. Every Christian should and must remain faithful to his own convictions, while, at the same time, respecting the convictions of others and praying that both he and all others may come to know more fully and to perform more exactly the will of

Christ. Sincere prayer of this type cannot but receive the blessing and the love of God.

On the part of Catholics, remaining true to their convictions that Mary is, under Christ, the Mediatress of all graces, there should be special prayers asking her, especially under the title of Lady of Perpetual Help, to intercede with the Godhead for an outflow of the gifts of knowledge, of understanding, and of charity.

In the Near East there live millions of people who belong to the . . . "Orthodox Church." . . . these Christians have always had a special love for the Mother of God and they are attracted to her under the title of Perpetual Help. "The popularity of the picture of Our Lady of Perpetual Help is not limited to the Catholics of the Oriental Rites but is also found among 'the Separated Peoples,' " writes Rev. John Corrigan, Assistant Secretary of the Catholic Near East Welfare Association. The Vicars of Christ, therefore, have made use of Our Lady of Perpetual Help in their efforts to bring . . . these . . . sheep to the one true fold.[2]

In addition to begging the intercession of the Mother of God, there should be earnest and continuous prayer to three men who lived before Christianity was torn asunder. They are honored in both the East and the West as masters of orthodoxy and of sanctity: St. Gregory Nazianzen (patriarch of Constantinople, 379-381), St. John Chrysostom (patriarch of Constantinople, 398-404), and St. Gregory the Great (papal legate at the court of Constantinople,

579-585; pope, 590-604). The council has been very fittingly entrusted to their patronage.

Yet, while Christians pray for the early advent of the unity which is the will of Christ, they must not forget another very clear directive of the same Shepherd: "The kingdom of heaven will not give entrance to every man who calls me Master, Master; only to the man that does the will of my Father who is in heaven." [3]

Prayer is good; it is essential, but it must be accompanied by action. There must be a real effort to live the life of the Gospel.

For a Catholic, with his convictions about the Living Mystical Body of Christ, the need for action is especially demanding. He knows that the Church is the Body of Christ, who is its Head. The two must go together. Bodies without heads and heads without bodies regularly achieve nothing. Not only do the members of Christ's Church depend on Him, but He wills to depend on the members: "The head (cannot say) to the feet, I have no need of you." [4]

It is true that Christ *could* have distributed His redemptive graces to the world without using any human instruments at all, without founding any Church. But He *did* found one, and He willed that all of its members should take part in spreading His teaching and commandments.

"This union with Our Lord in the Church is not a solely personal affair; it does not end with making ourselves better, though it will begin there. It is union with Christ as He is: Christ, the *Source of Grace,* but also the *Fisher of Men,*" and also the *Good Shepherd* who wants all His sheep in *one* fold, "and thus it places upon all certain obligations actually to do something for building up the Body of Christ," the Sheepfold. "If the world is going to be saved," if Christians are going to be united, "it is the concern of *every* member of Christ's Mystical Body; the divine head has need of everyone of them. Whether they be working in offices or factories, teaching or studying in schools, caring for the sick or managing a home, they are called upon to help Christ in that particular place where they are." [5]

At present, Christ is calling to all the members of His Mystical Body to help Him to bring all Christians to a true unity of true faith.

It is not enough for them simply to pray for unity, to speak of Christ's teaching about unity. They must "above all, mirror Christ in their lives. They have to 'put on Christ.' They have to *be* Christ in all they are, in all they do and say." [6] If with their tongues and in their behavior they repeatedly wound their Christian neighbors or give bad example, if their life at home and in the family is pagan and disunited, they have no reason to expect that their prayers for unity will have any effect.

In summary, then, both the prayer and the activity of all Christians—whether they think of themselves as members of Christ's Mystical Body or not—are necessary, if the council's work for the promotion of unity among Christians is to have any success. The prayers must be never-ending, and the activity ever zealous, ever charitable. Christ wants it that way. He has made Himself, His work, and the unity of His Church dependent upon human beings—upon you and me! It is a serious thought, a shocking thought! But a truth which should become a moving force in our lives! [7]

OFFICIAL PRAYER FOR SUCCESS
OF COUNCIL [8]

"O Divine Spirit who, sent by the Father in the name of Jesus, is present in the Church and guides it infallibly, benignly pour out Your gifts, we pray, upon the ecumenical council.

"Grant that abundant fruits may come from this council, that the light and force of the Gospel may be increasingly propagated in the society of man, that Catholic religious and fervent missionary works may flourish with increased vigor; that a more profound knowledge of the teaching of the Church may be attained and that Christian customs may achieve salutary progress.

"O sweet Guest of the Soul, make our minds firm in the truth and dispose our hearts to obedience, so that what is decided by the council may be welcomed with sincere respect and put into practice with a ready will.

"We also pray to You for those sheep who do not belong to the one sheepfold of Christ, so that they too may ultimately achieve unity under the government of one single Shepherd and glory in the Christian name.

"Renew Your wonders in our time, as though for a new Pentecost, and grant that the Holy Church, preserving unanimous and continuous prayer, together with Mary, the mother of Jesus, and also under the guidance of St. Peter, may increase the reign of the Divine Saviour, the reign of truth and justice, the reign of love and peace. Amen."

CHAPTER XVIII

Slow Haste

The opening of the council on January 25, 1962, leaves an interval of three years between the first announcement and the formal beginning. Actually, considering the amount of work which is entailed, such a length of time is not surprising. And yet one may hear such impatient questions as: what's taking all the time? why don't they hurry up?

Briefly, the time is being consumed by three things: 1. the complexity of all the problems which have to be studied; 2. the multiplicity of the delicate preparations which have to be made to insure a maximum degree of success; 3. the thoroughness of preparation which must be achieved in order to keep the length of the formal council as brief as possible lest the bishops of the world be forced to be absent from their dioceses for an extended period of time.

More specifically, in only one year, between two Pentecosts, much of the organizational work was done by an antepreparatory commission of twelve prelates chosen from among the various Congregations, Tribunals, and Offices which assist the Supreme Pontiff in the administration of the affairs of the Church.

Letters asking for suggestions were sent to about 2700 bishops and Church dignitaries. About eighty per cent replied in detail. Their suggestions were catalogued according to topics and subtopics on about 2100 file cards and were then synthesized according to national origin.

In a similar manner proposals were requested from the Roman Congregations. Theologians and canon law experts of Catholic universities around the world were asked to report their views. Again, all responses were filed according to general subject and subtopic.

Using the information from the card-index file, the commission went on to work out a general outline of the matters to be discussed by the council. Finally, it suggested the structure of the preparatory commissions and secretariats. They are: 1. a central commission, presided over by the Pope or by his cardinal legate, for coordinating the work of all the other commissions and secretariats, and for reporting to the Pope personally on the progress and conclusions being made; 2. a theological commission to deal with questions touching Holy Scripture, sacred traditions, the Faith and its practices; 3. a commission for the bishops and diocesan government; 4. a commission dealing with regulations for clergy and faithful; 5. a commission dealing with matters for religious; 6. a commission on regulating the sacraments; 7. a commission on sacred liturgy; 8. a commission on studies and seminaries; 9. a commission for the Eastern Churches; 10. a commission for the missions; 11. a commission for the lay apostolate in religious and social fields; 12. a secretariat for the media of communication (press, radio, television, motion pictures, etc.); 13. a secretariat, or "advisory board," to aid all Christians who are not in communion with the Holy See to follow the work of the council and to find more easily the path to Christian unity; 14. a secretariat for the economic affairs of the council; 15. a secretariat for the technical aspects of the council. Finally, if the need arises, the Pope may establish still other commissions, while those already established may create their own subcommissions.

Fundamentally, the reason for all the intricate organization and careful preparation lies, quite simply, in the fact that the Catholic Church has some very old doctrines to protect and to hand on, teachings that were entrusted to her in the very springtime of her youth, teachings which she was told to guard until her Founder should come again. This she has done. This she will do, faithfully proposing them in each new era, making her words and actions intelligible to each new generation.

Hers is a sacred duty, a God-given work—one that she cannot afford to bungle with haste. Every statement, every proposition has to check out with the facts. Even though she can rely on the continued help of her Founder, still she has the obligation of bringing to her work all the care and prudence of which human genius is capable. Anything less would be unworthy of her mission of shepherding all the nations.

As time goes on and on, hers is a task which is ever old, yet ever new. And it seems to be a fact that, as the years reel off into chains of centuries, only the very young and the very old, those who are closest to the timeless unhurriedness of God, can—and do—refuse to be hurried. The Catholic Church is both: very young and very old.

All Scripture quotations are from THE HOLY BIBLE in the translation of Monsignor Ronald Knox, Copyright 1950, Sheed and Ward, Inc., New York.

Foreword

1. P. Parente, A. Piolanti, and S. Garofalo, *Dictionary of Dogmatic Theology* (Milwaukee: Bruce, 1951), p. vii.

Introduction

1. J. M. Todd, *Catholicism and the Ecumenical Movement* (New York: Longmans, Green and Co., 1956), pp. 22-66.
2. G. H. Tavard, *The Catholic Approach to Protestantism* (New York: Harper and Bros., 1955), pp. 116-142.

Chapter I

1. Tavard, *op. cit.*, pp. 62, 63.
2. I Corinthians 13: 4-7.

Chapter II

1. S. H. Butcher, *Some Aspects of Greek Genius.* 3rd edit. (London: Macmillan, 1904), p. 188.

Chapter III

1. There have been three plenary councils in the United States. They were held at Baltimore in 1852, 1866 and 1884.

Chapter V

1. Cf. John 21: 15-17.
2. Cf. Matthew 16: 16-19.
3. J. Hardouin, *Collectio maxima conciliorum generalium et provincialium* (Paris, 1715), Vol. I, col. 1346.
4. *Ibid.,* Vol. II, col. 71.
5. An example of the very clear understanding of this relation of Pope and emperor in calling a council is to be found in a letter of Pope Leo the Great in reference to the Council of Chalcedon, held under him in 451: "the general council was pleased to gather both from the command of the Christian princes and from the consent of the Apostolic See." Migne, *Patrologia Latina* (Paris: Garnier, 1881), Vol. 54, col. 1029.

Chapter VI

1. It must, of course, be remembered, that misunderstandings and misinterpretations can be permitted by Divine Providence without a violation of infallibility. At the same time—through the sanctity which they engender as a result of humble and obedient acceptance—they can bring greater glory to God. It is God's glory which is the first purpose of all creation.
2. Migne, *op. cit.,* col. 951.

Chapter VIII

1. Matthew 28: 16-20, And now the eleven disciples took their journey into Galilee, to the mountain where Jesus had bidden them meet him. When they saw him there, they fell down to worship; though some were still doubtful. But Jesus came near and spoke to them; All authority in heaven and on earth, he said, has been given to me; you, therefore, must go out, making disciples of all nations, and baptizing them in the name of the Father, and of the Son, and of the Holy Ghost, teaching them to observe all the commandments which I have given you. And behold I am with you all through the days that are coming, until the consummation of the world.

Mark 16: 14-16: Then at last he appeared to all eleven of them as they sat at table, and reproached them with their unbelief and their obstinacy of heart, in giving no credit to those who had seen him after he had risen. And he said to them, Go out all over the world, and preach the gospel to the whole of creation; he who believes and is baptized will be saved; he who refuses belief will be condemned.

For the choosing of the Twelve Apostles see Mark 3: 13 and Luke 6: 12.

2. For an infallible papal pronouncement, four conditions have to be fulfilled: a. The Pope has to be speaking as universal shepherd and teacher, b. on matters of faith and morals, c. in a definitive statement, d. through which he clearly shows his intention of demanding the assent of the whole flock.

Chapter IX

1. John 14: 16-17.
2. John 16: 12-13.

3. Matthew 28: 18-20.

4. Mark 16: 16.

5. Confer Matthew 16: 17-19; John 21: 15-18.

6. Mark 16: 16.

7. According to Catholic belief each of the Apostles enjoyed the gift of *personal* infallibility, but it was an *extraordinary* assistance given in view of the special needs of the early Church. Therefore, it was not granted to each of their successors.

8. R. J. Bellarmine, *De Conciliis,* I, 17, as quoted in E. S. Berry, *The Church of Christ.* 2nd edit. (Gettysburg: Times and News Publishing Co., 1955), p. 261.

9. E. S. Berry, *ibid.*

Chapter XI

1. J. Forget, *Dictionnaire de Théologie Catholique* (Paris: Letouzey et Ané, 1938), Vol. III, "Conciles," col. 668.

2. T. Zapelena, *De Ecclesia Christi* (Rome: Gregorian University, 1954), II, 180-181.

3. G. Van Noort, trans. and revised by J. J. Castelot and W. R. Murphy, *Christ's Church* (Westminster, Md.: Newman Press, 1957), p. 333.

4. Bellarmine, *op. cit.,* as quoted in Berry, *op. cit.,* p. 237.

5. Canon 224.

6. Van Noort, *op. cit.,* p. 333.

Chapter XII

1. Canon 226.

2. Canon 222.

3. Canon 225.

4. Canon 227.

5. Canon 229.
6. Canon 228.
7. Van Noort, *op. cit.,* p. 337.
8. Forget, *op. cit.,* col. 670.

Chapter XIII

1. In the nineteenth century Protestants began to use the word *ecumenical* when referring to the world-wide missionary endeavor of the Church. During the early decades of the twentieth century the term designated matters of interaction and of unity between different Christian Churches or their members. It is now applied by Protestants to any action of world-wide scope which gives evidence of a longing for and an awareness of the need for the full unity which Christ intended that His Church should have. Cf. G. Weigel, *A Catholic Primer on the Ecumenical Movement* (Westminster, Md.: Newman Press, 1958).

2. Acts 15: 28.

3. C. J. Hefele, *A History of the Christian Councils,* trans. and edited by W. R. Clark (Edinburgh: T. & T. Clark, 1871), I, 1.

4. Eusebius, *Church History,* Book V, chap. 16, according to Hefele, *op. cit.,* p. 77.

Chapter XIV

1. Cf. Hefele-Leclerq, *Histoire des Conciles,* I, 1-124; Forget, *op. cit.,* cols. 670-674; C. Raab, *The Twenty Ecumenical Councils* (Westminster, Md.: Newman Press, 1959); J. McSorley, *Outline History of the Church by Centuries,* 10th newly revised edition (St. Louis: Herder, 1957).

2. The fifteenth chapter of *Acts* tells of an assembly of

Apostles and presbyters which was held at Jerusalem about the year 49. It was a council, but it was not ecumenical. First, it was a meeting of only the Church of Jerusalem. There is no indication that they thought of themselves as representing the whole Church. Secondly, while the decisions did have a doctrinal character and did ultimately receive universal acceptance, they were not published as definitive decrees which were to be binding upon the whole Church. The assembled Apostles and presbyters of the Church of Jerusalem made definite decisions, but they intended them immediately only as answers to questions from the Christian community at Antioch.

Chapter XV

1. Confer Ephesians 4: 2-6; I Corinthians 12; Colossians 1: 18; Romans 12: 3-21.

2. Bossuet, in J. C. Gruden, *The Mystical Christ* (St. Louis: Herder, 1938), p. 2.

3. John 17: 21.

Chapter XVI

1. The list of possible council considerations which is presented is not intended in any way to anticipate the judgment of the Fathers of the council. All examples are adduced merely for the purpose of clarification. They are not intended in any way to suggest that the council would be remiss in not considering the examples mentioned.

2. In God's plan for the redemption of mankind the Blessed Mother of our Lord occupies, in some respects, a position similar to that of a hospital nurse. At one time a nurse may assist a doctor directly, or even aid him in the preparation of a medicine, while at another time she

distributes those medicines to the patients. These two duties of assistance and distribution correspond roughly to Mary's offices of Co-Redemptress and Mediatress.

On the one hand she worked with her Son in the preparation of grace. She is Co-Redemptress, "redeeming with him" (Pius XI), because she freely consented to become the Mother of God and also freely offered her Son as a Victim on Calvary. Of course, this co-redeeming was possible to her only in subordination to her Son and to His redeeming power; it was possible only because she herself was already redeemed by Him, and, in fact, already enjoying the fruits of redemption.

On the other hand, she is the Mediatress of all graces and now distributes all graces to mankind. Anyone would admit that it is proper for one who has earned the gifts of grace to receive the right of distributing them. Thus, God, recognizing that propriety, after having allowed Mary to cooperate in meriting all the graces of the redemption, has now placed all of them at her disposal, so that she may distribute them to a needy world. Confer: Feckes, *The Mystery of the Divine Motherhood* (Spiritual Book Associates, N. Y., 1941), pp. 163-183.

3. J. A. M. Quigley, *Proceedings of the Twelfth Annual Convention of the Catholic Theological Society of America,* "The Changing Concept of Servile Work" (New York, 1958), pp. 145-155.

4. R. A. Graham, "Will Christians Come Together?" *America,* C (February 28, 1959).

5. Cf. R. J. Miller, "All Roads Lead to Rome in 1961," *Liguorian,* 47 (September, 1959).

Chapter XVII

1. Matthew 28: 20.

2. S. McKenna, *Everyone's Madonna* (Boston: Mission Church Press, 1941), p. 34.

3. Matthew 7: 21.

4. I Corinthians 12: 21.

5. J. Murphy, *The Living Christ* (Milwaukee: Bruce, 1952), p. 152.

6. *Ibid.*, p. 153.

7. *Ibid.*

8. *Acta Apostolicae Sedis,* quoted in *The Witness* (Dubuque, Ia., January 7, 1960).

Adam, K. *One and Holy*. New York: Sheed and Ward, 1951.

—— *The Spirit of Catholicism*. New York: Macmillan, 1953.

Algermissen, K. *Christian Denominations*. St. Louis, Mo.: Herder, 1945.

Attwater, D. *Eastern Catholic Worship*. New York: Devin-Adair, 1945.

—— *The Christian Churches of the East*. 2 vols. Milwaukee: Bruce, 1947.

Baum, G. *That They May Be One; a Study of Papal Doctrine* (Leo XIII–Pius XII). Westminster, Md.: Newman Press, 1958.

Bell, G. K. A., ed., *Documents on Christian Unity*. 3rd series: 1930-48. London: Oxford University Press, 1948.

Billot, L. *De Ecclesia Christi*. Rome: Gregorian University, 15th ed., 1927.

Bouyer, L. *The Spirit and Forms of Protestantism.* Trans. by A. V. Littledale. Westminster, Md.: Newman Press, 1956.

Boyer, C. *One Shepherd.* Trans. by Angeline Bouchard. New York: P. J. Kenedy and Sons, 1952.

Cary-Elwes, C. *The Sheepfold and the Shepherd.* New York: Longmans, Green and Co., 1956.

Chapman, J. *The First Eight General Councils and Papal Infallibility.* London: Catholic Truth Society, 1908.

Congar, Y. *Divided Christendom.* London: Geofrey Bles, 1947.

De Lubac, H. *Catholicism.* London: Burns, Oates, and Washbourne, 1950.

Dolan, T. *The Papacy and the First Councils of the Church.* St. Louis, Mo.: Herder, 1910.

Fliche, A.–Martin, V. *Histoire de l'Église.* 17 vols. Paris: Bloud & Gay, 1946- ──.

Forget, J. *Dictionnaire Apologétique de la Foi Catholique,* "Conciles." Paris: Beauchesne et C., 1911.

────── *Dictionnaire de Théologie Catholique,* Tome 3-A, "Conciles." Paris: Letouzey et Ané, 1938.

Fortescue, A. *The Orthodox Eastern Church.* London: Catholic Truth Society, 1907.

Gordillo, M. *Compendium Theologia Orientalis,* 2nd ed. Rome: Pont. Institutum Orientalium Studiorum, 1939.

Gruden, J. *The Mystical Christ.* St. Louis: Herder, 1938.

Haddan, A. *Dictionary of Christian Antiquities,* Vol. 1, "Council." London: Murray, 1908.

Hanahoe, E. *Catholic Ecumenism.* Washington, D. C.: Catholic University Press, 1953.

Hanahoe-Cranny, eds., *One Fold.* Graymoor, Garrison, N.Y.: Chair of Unity Apostolate, 1960.

Hanulya, J. *The Eastern Ritual.* Cleveland, 1950.

Hardon, J. *The Protestant Churches of America.* Westminster, Md.: Newman Press, 1956.

—— *Christianity in Conflict.* Westminster, Md.: Newman Press, 1959.

Hardouin, J. *Collectio maxima conciliorum generalium et provincialium.* 13 vols. Paris: 1715-1722.

Hauch, A. *Schaff-Herzog Religious Encyclopedia,* Vol. 3, "Councils and Synods." New York: Funk and Wagnalls, 1909.

Hefele, C. *A History of the Christian Councils.* 5 vols. Edinburgh: T. & T. Clark, 1871-1896.

Hefele–de Clercq. *Histoire des Conciles.* 11 vols. Paris: Librairie Letouzey et Ané, 1907-1952.

Henry, A. *Introduction to Theology.* Chicago: Fides, 1954.

Hervé, J. *Manuale Theologiae Dogmaticae,* Vol. I, "De Ecclesia Christi." Paris: Berche et Pagis, 1957.

Hughes, P. *A Popular History of the Reformation.* Garden City, N.Y.: Hanover House, 1957.

Janin, R. *The Separated Eastern Churches.* St. Louis, Mo.: Herder, 1933.

Jedin, H. *Ecumenical Councils in the Catholic Church.* New York: Herder and Herder, 1960.

John XXIII, Pope. *On Truth, Unity and Peace* (encyclical letter of June 29, 1959). New York: America Press, 1959.

Journet, C. *The Church of the Word Incarnate.* New York: Sheed and Ward, 1955.

—— *The Primacy of Peter from the Protestant and from the Catholic Point of View.* Westminster, Md.: Newman Press, 1954.

Kane, J. *Catholic-Protestant Conflicts in America.* Chicago: Regnery, 1955.

Kenrick, F. *The Primacy of the Apostolic See and the Authority of the General Councils.* Philadelphia: Kay and Bros., 1838.

King, A. *The Rites of Eastern Christendom.* 2 vols. London: Burns, Oates and Washbourne, 1950.

Krafft, K. *Kirchliche Wiederbereinigung.* Mainz: Rupferberg, 1871.

Lannert, J. *The Reunion of Christendom.* St. Meinrad, Ind.: Abbey Press, 1932.

Leclercq, H. *Dictionnaire d'Archéologie Chrétienne et de Liturgie,* Tome 13, "Conciles." Paris: Letouzey et Ané, 1914.

Lemonnyer, A. *Dictionnaire de la Bible, Supplement,* Tome 2, "Concile de Jérusalem." Paris: Letouzey et Ané, 1934.

McGarrigle, A. *The Eastern Branches of the Catholic Church.* New York: Longmans, Green, and Co., 1936.

McSorley, J. *Outline History of the Church by Centuries,* 10th ed. St. Louis, Mo.: Herder, 1957.

Murphy, J. *The General Councils of the Church.* Milwaukee: Bruce, 1960.

Palmieri, D. *De Romano Pontifice.* Rome: Ex Typographia Polyglotta, 1877.

Pius XII, Pope. *Discorsi e Radiomessaggi di Sua Santità,* Vol. VII, "Nel Quarto Centenario del Concilio di Trento." Milano: Vita e Pensiero, 1946.

Raab, C. *The Twenty Ecumenical Councils of the Catholic Church.* Westminster, Md.: Newman Press, 1959.

Salaverri, J. *Sacrae Theologiae Summa,* Vol. I, "De Ecclesia Christi," 3rd ed. Madrid: B.A.C., 1955.

Schneider, E. *Lexikon für Theologie und Kirche,* Vol. 6, "Konzil." Freiburg/Breisgau: Herder, 1934.

Segur, P. *Das Concil, Ein Büchlein für das katholische Volk*. Mainz: Kirchheim, 1869.

Spirit of Christian Unity, The (a series of eight papers setting forth the Catholic attitude toward the reunion of Christendom). Oxford: Blackfriars, 1950.

St. John, H. *Essays in Christian Unity*. Westminster, Md.: Newman Press, 1955.

Tanquerey-Bord. *Synopsis Theologiae Dogmaticae Fundamentalis*, Vol. I, "De Vera Christi Ecclesia," ed. 26. Paris: Desclée et Socii, 1949.

Tavard, G. *The Catholic Approach to Protestantism*. New York: Harper and Bros., 1955.

—— *Holy Writ or Holy Church: the Crisis of the Protestant Reformation*. New York: Harper, 1960.

—— *Protestant Hopes and the Catholic Responsibility*. Notre Dame, Ind.: Fides Publishers, 1960.

—— *Protestantism*. New York: Hawthorn, 1959.

Todd, J. *Catholicism and the Ecumenical Movement*. New York: Longmans, Green and Co., 1956.

Van de Pol, W. *The Christian Dilemma*. New York: Philosophical Library, 1952.

Van Doornik–Jelsma–Van de Lisdonk. *A Handbook of the Catholic Faith*. New York: Image Books, 1956.

Van Noort, G. *Christ's Church*. Trans. and rev. by J. J. Castelot and W. R. Murphy. Westminster, Md.: Newman Press, 1957.

Weigel, G. *A Catholic Primer on the Ecumenical Movement*. Westminster, Md.: Newman Press, 1958.

—— *A Survey of Protestant Theology in Our Day*. Westminster, Md.: Newman Press, 1954.

—— *Faith and Understanding in America*. New York: Macmillan, 1959.

Wilhelm, J. *The Catholic Encyclopedia,* Vol. 4, "General Councils." New York: The Encyclopedia Press, 1913.

Zapelena, T. *De Ecclesia Christi.* 2 vols. Rome: Gregorian University, 1950-1954.

Periodicals:

At-ONE-ment. Monastery of the Atonement, Washington, D. C.

Eastern Churches Quarterly, The. Catholic Near East, New York 17, N. Y.

Irenikon. Benedictine Priory, Chevetogne, Belgium.

One Church. Russian Orthodox Periodical, New York, N. Y.

Unitas. Gregorian University, Rome (Eng. ed.: Graymoor Press, Peekskill, N. Y.).

The Voice of the Church. St. Procopius Abbey, Lisle, Illinois.

ABBOT (Aramaic: *abba,* father)—The superior or father of a monastery or abbey.

ABBOT-GENERAL—The chief abbot of a monastic order, i.e., of a group of monasteries which have the same rule of life.

ADOPTIONISM—A heresy which taught that Christ was only the adopted son of God, not the true Son of God the Father.

APOLOGETIC MIRACLE—A miracle which is worked for the purpose of proving that a statement or revelation is true.

APOSTOLATE (Greek: *apostolos,* one sent forth)—The office and activity of one who is sent on a mission, especially the mission of spreading the Gospel.

APOSTOLIC COLLEGE—The twelve Apostles plus St. Paul.

ARCHBISHOP (Greek: *archein,* to be first; *episkopus,* overseer)—A bishop of first rank. See TITULAR ARCHBISHOP and METROPOLITAN (ARCHBISHOP).

ARCHDIOCESE—The territory which is under the religious rule of an archbishop.

ARIANISM—A heresy which denied the divinity of the Word. Thus the Trinity was denied too.

AUXILIARY BISHOP—A coadjutor bishop who does not have the right of succession.

BENEDICTION—A blessing, especially the solemn blessing which is imparted by tracing the Sign of the Cross before an assembled congregation with the Sacred Body of Christ, really present in the consecrated Eucharist.

BISHOP (Greek: *episkopus,* an overseer)—A man who is a successor of the Apostles. He becomes such when he receives the fullness of the priesthood through consecration by another bishop.

CANON (Greek: *kanon,* rule or rod)—A law, definition, or decree about a matter of Christian doctrine or discipline.

CANON LAW—The group of 2414 canons according to which the Church is governed.

CLOISTER (Latin: *claudere,* to close)—That part of a religious order, life, or house which is closed off from the distractions of the world.

COADJUTOR BISHOP—A titular bishop who has been assigned by the Holy See to assist the residential bishop of a diocese. There are three classes: 1. those assigned to the person of the bishop, with the right to succeed him in office; 2. those assigned to the person of the bishop without the right to succeed him in office (auxiliary bishops in the strict sense); 3. those assigned to the diocese.

COUNCIL—See pp. 15 ff.; also pp. 86 and 87.

DIOCESE—The territory which is under the religious rule of a residential bishop.

DOGMA (Greek: *dokein,* to think, believe)—A doctrine or the body of doctrines which the faithful are obliged to believe because they are truths which have been revealed by God and are taught as such by the Church.

DOGMATIC RELATIVISM—The false idea that the truth of a dogma depends upon its relation to current philosophy, scientific advance, etc.

EASTER CONTROVERSY—A second-century difficulty which arose from the fact that in Rome the feast of Easter was celebrated on the Sunday following the March full moon, while in Asia Minor there was an Apostolic tradition of celebrating it on the fourteenth day of the Jewish month of Nisan (March-April). Some of the bishops of Asia Minor found it difficult to comply when the Bishop of Rome ordered them to follow the Roman custom.

ECCLESIASTICAL (Greek: *ekklesia,* an assembly, a church)—Of, or pertaining to a church.

ECCLESIOLOGY—A branch of learning which deals with churches. It may refer to the externals of art, adornment, and antiquity; or it may be a theological study of the inner nature of a church as a divine institution.

ECUMENICAL (pronounced: ek-kew-MEN-i-k'l)— World-wide. Of, or pertaining to the whole world. Universal. In the phrase *ecumenical council,* as used by Catholics, it means a council of all the churches of the world which are in communion with the Holy See. In the phrase *ecumenical movement,* and as the word is used in general by Protestants, it means that which promotes the world-wide unity which Christ intends for all Christians. See pages 86-88.

ECUMENICITY—1. (in reference to an ecumenical council) The quality of representing and/or of having binding authority upon the whole Church. 2. (in reference to the ecumenical movement) The world-wide unity which Christ intended for all Christians.

ECUMENIST—One who promotes matters which aid in achieving the full world-wide unity which Christ intended for all Christians.

ENCYCLICAL (Greek: *en,* in; *kyklos,* circle)—A letter addressed by the pope to the bishops of the world, in general, or to those in a large area of the world.

EPISCOPAL COLLEGE—The bishops of the Church.

EXEGETE (Greek: *exegeisthai,* to interpret)—One who is skilled in explaining, especially the Bible.

FEUDALISTIC—Pertaining to the system of feudalism, the social, political, and economic system of the Middle Ages.

FORTY-HOURS' DEVOTION—A devotion of forty hours' duration during which Christ really present in the Eucharist is placed openly on the altar and given special adoration.

HERESY (Greek: *hairein,* to take, select)—The selection, by a baptized person, of the revealed doctrines which he will accept. Conversely, the denial of any publicly revealed truth which is taught by the Church.

HIERARCHY (Greek: *hieros,* sacred; *archein,* to rule)— The body of persons who have been chosen by God, at least indirectly, to lead and to rule in the Church.

HOLY SEE (Latin: *sedes,* a seat, i.e., of authority)—The pope and all the congregations, tribunals, offices, and commissions by which he governs the affairs of the whole Church.

ICONOCLASM (Greek: *eikon,* image; *klastos,* broken into pieces)—A heresy which taught that all religious use of images or statues is wrong, and that they are to be destroyed.

INFALLIBILITY—Freedom from error. See Chapters IX and X.

IRENICISM (Greek: *eirene,* peace)—Pacificism. The spirit of conciliation.

JURISDICTION (Latin: *juris,* of the law; *dictio,* a saying, speaking)—Legal power to govern, legislate, or control.

JUSTIFICATION—The act of becoming free or the state of being free from all serious sin and deliberate attachment to serious sin so as to possess God's sanctifying grace, love and friendship.

KNIGHTS TEMPLAR—A military-religious order founded during the Crusades (1118) to care for pilgrims in the Holy Land.

LAITY—All persons who are not numbered among the clergy. Laymen.

LEGATE—A representative. An envoy. An ambassador.

MACEDONIANISM—A heresy which denied the divinity of the Holy Spirit.

What Is An

MARIOLOGY—The branch of theology which deals with doctrinal truths that pertain to Mary, the Mother of God.

METROPOLITAN (ARCHBISHOP) (Greek: *meter,* mother; *polis,* city)—An archbishop who has full religious authority over his own diocese and limited authority over one or more additional dioceses.

MONOPHYSITISM (Greek: *monos,* alone; *physis,* nature)—A heresy which taught that there was one person and only one nature in Christ after the Incarnation, the human nature being absorbed by the divine. The truth is that Christ had a divine nature and a human nature, both of which remained unmixed and unconfused.

MONOTHELITISM (Greek: *monos,* alone; *thelema,* will)—A heresy which taught that Christ had only a divine will. The truth is that, having a complete human nature, he had a human will too.

MONTANISM—A second-century heresy which taught that one Montanus had received the third and last revelation, that of the Holy Spirit. It also maintained that the second coming of Christ was close at hand.

MORAL PERSON—A juridical being, such as a corporation, which is established by a competent authority. It is distinct from all physical or natural persons.

MORAL UNANIMITY—An agreement or consent which is virtually or practically complete.

MYSTICAL BODY—In the revealed sense used by St. Paul, and as explained by Pius XII in his encyclical *Mystici Corporis:* the Catholic Church which is juridically united with the successor of St. Peter.

NESTORIANISM—A heresy which maintained that there were two persons and two natures in Christ and that Mary was the mother of the human person. Actually, there are in Christ two natures, one human and one divine; but there is only one person, which is divine. A mother is the mother of the whole person. Therefore Mary is the Mother of God.

ORTHODOX (Greek: *orthos,* correct; *doxa,* opinion)— 1. Proper. Correct. Accepted. Usual. 2. (when capitalized) The Greek Orthodox Church, which maintains that it holds the faith which was stated in the great creeds and councils of the early Church. But it rejects the authority of the Roman See.

PATRIARCH (Greek: *pater,* father; *archein,* to be first) —An honorary title given to those archbishops who govern certain important dioceses. The archbishops of Venice and Lisbon are patriarchs, as is the highest ranking bishop of the various Eastern Catholic, or Uniat, Churches. The Catholic archbishops of Jerusalem, Antioch, Alexandria, and Istanbul (Constantinople) are *Greater Patriarchs,* while the pope is the *Patriarch of the West.*

POLYGENISM—The theory that the human race has descended from more than one original couple. Pope Pius XII, in his encyclical *Humani Generis,* stated that it is in no way apparent how the theory can be made to agree with the revealed truth that original sin has come to all mankind from one human being.

PRELATE—A high-ranking dignitary in the Church, e.g., a bishop.

PRESBYTER (Greek: *presbyteros,* an old man)—An elder person. In the early Church the term was used interchangeably of laymen, priests, and bishops.

PRIMATE—An honorary title which is given to an archbishop whose predecessors in former centuries had religious authority over several archdioceses, or even over whole countries.

PROVINCE—The group of dioceses over which a metropolitan archbishop has religious authority.

RESIDENTIAL BISHOP—A bishop who is placed over a particular territory, called a diocese. He governs the religious affairs of the diocese under the religious authority of the pope.

ROMAN CURIA—The group of sacred congregations, tribunals, and offices which help the pope to govern the Church.

ROMAN OFFICE—One of several permanent bodies which assist the pope especially in ministerial matters of Church government, e.g., transactions between the Holy See and civil powers.

ROMAN TRIBUNAL—One of three permanent bodies which aid the pope in governing the Church, particularly in a judicial capacity.

SACRED CONGREGATION—One of several permanent bodies or committees which aid the Roman Pontiff in governing the Church, particularly in an administrative and executive capacity.

SCHISM (Greek: *schizein,* to split)—A formal splitting away from the Catholic Church by refusing to accept the jurisdiction of the pope.

SIMONY—Buying or selling spiritual items or positions in the Church.

SUPERIOR-GENERAL—The chief superior of a religious congregation.

SYNOD—An ecclesiastical council, especially one which is limited to the bishop and the clergy of one diocese. See also Chapter XIII, p. 86.

THEOLOGY (Greek: *theos,* god; *logos,* discourse)—The science or systematic study of God and the things of God.

TITULAR ARCHBISHOP—An archbishop who has authority over only one diocese, or who bears the title of a region which is now no longer Catholic.

TITULAR BISHOP—A bishop who has received the fullness of the priesthood but has not been given the right to govern the religious affairs of the diocese whose title he bears.

TRANSEPT—Either the right or the left arm of a church which is built in the form of a cross.

TRANSUBSTANTIATION—The changing of the substance of bread into the substance of the Body of Christ and the substance of wine into the substance of the Blood of Christ by the words of consecration at Mass so that only the appearances of bread and wine remain.

USURY—An excessive rate of interest charged on a loan.

VULGATE (Latin: *vulgatus,* common)—The standard Latin version of the Bible which was given special approbation by the Council of Trent and which, for the most part, is the translation of St. Jerome, dating from the late fourth and early fifth centuries.

Index

A NOTE ON THE TYPE

IN WHICH THIS BOOK IS SET

This book is set in Times Roman, a Linotype face created by Stanley Morrison, world-famous typographical authority. It was designed for the London *Times,* which demanded a type face that should be clear and legible, precise but not mechanical, having a high letter but not condensed, of a "color" suitable for any paper or printing process, with character but not with annoying characteristics. The clear, open characters of Times Roman are the secret of its clear printing on any paper, whether it be on the coarsest of newsprint or the finest coated paper. This book was composed and printed by the Wickersham Printing Company of Lancaster, Pa., and bound by Moore and Company of Baltimore. Typography and design are by Howard N. King.